Men Cheat Women Experiment

Men Cheat Women Experiment

A Novel by
Natosha Gale Lewis

Published by K.D. Publishing
Distributed by
A&B Distributors
1000 Atlantic Avenue
Brooklyn, New York 11238
718.783.7808

Write4life Productions
Visit: www.NatoshaGaleLewis.com

Published by **Write4life Productions**
P.O. Box 12723, Wilmington, DE 19850

Third Printing, March 2005

Lewis, Natosha Gale
Men Cheat Women Experiment/by Natosha Gale Lewis.
p.cm.
ISBN: 0-9723049-4-0

1. Adult-Fiction.I. Title

Printed in the United States of America.

People often ask me at various events, "So, is this your life story?" My answer to this question is always a resounding, "No, this is not my life."

Dedication

The book, like my entire life is dedicated to the sweetest child alive, my daughter, Courtney. I also dedicate this book to my very best friend, my mother. Thank you both for sharing my world.

"I trust you with my life but never with my heart."
—Natosha Gale Lewis

Chapter1

Xavier

I love my wife and wouldn't trade her for a million dollars—make it two and I just might consider leaving. Stacey and I have been married for twelve years. We have two children, Justin, twelve, and Ayanna, two. Like most married couples, we have our share of problems, but for the most part, I'm pretty content, as long as I can just be me.

Stacey and I recently got back together. We're both employed by the Philadelphia Police Department, otherwise known as Philadelphia's Finest. I recently got promoted to detective. This job can be extremely detrimental to a marriage; trust me, I know from firsthand experience. Stacey never wanted to be a cop. It's bad enough that I was one, but then three years ago, Stacey lost her computer job at one of those dot-com companies. She had taken the police officer's exam about four years ago, and when the department went on a mad hiring frenzy and was looking for people, especially minorities and females, Stacey was pretty much what they were looking for. She has a bachelor's degree in computer science, so thank God, she was assigned to the police administration building

BEWARE OF DOG!

after only working on the streets for two years. Now I say "thank God" for a number of reasons. First, let me get this straight: Skirts don't belong on the street. There's only one thing worse than a female cop and that's two female cops. Don't get me wrong, I love women, but I can't stand female cops! The other reason I didn't want Stacey to become a cop was because I knew that was going to severely mess up my game plan. I'm just gon' put it out there. I love being a playa playa. Married or not, I'm never giving up my playa's card.

You know male cops get so much play it should be a felony. Wearing that uniform, trust me when I tell you, women just be throwing the pussy at you. What's a man to do? But, I'm here to tell you that there must be a God, because last year, Stacey was involved in a car accident. She didn't get hurt too badly, just messed up her back a little. While she was on limited duty, they temporarily assigned her to police headquarters and that's when some big-shot found out that she had that computer science background. Next thing you know Stacey was permanently assigned downtown. That was good news to my ears. See, having Stacey on the street and learning my game was not good for me. So, now that Stacey is downtown, she has set hours and that means she doesn't get to move around the city, meeting other female cops who would probably run their damn mouths to Stacey about all the things that I'm out there doing. You know women don't know how to shut the hell up. They always like to just keep yap, yap, yapping. Next thing you know, Stacey will be all up in my business.

Until recently, I was all set. I had this nice little honey on the side. Jasmine Goodson. Who could forget that damn tongue ring and all the tricks she did with that? Man, I almost got caught up for a minute. Well, actually, I did. You see,

BEWARE OF DOG!

Jasmine lives out on City Line Avenue in this nice little condo. She was built just like I like them. You know, cute in the face and tight in the waist. Honey had it goin' on. No kids, good job, no man and good in bed. I used to work the rotation shift. Two weeks on 8:00 AM to 4:00 PM and then two weeks on 4:00 PM to 12:00 AM, but then I got wise and volunteered for the 12:00 AM to 8:00 AM shift. Stacey and I usually work together to get the kids bathed and in bed. By the time 9:00 PM rolls around, Stacey is so beat that she can't normally keep her eyes opened. That's when I get my creep on and roll on over to Jasmine's before work. Sometimes, when the loving was really good, I would call off from work and sleep over Jasmine's. Now that made both of us happy.

I remember the first time I met Jas. She had on these little jean shorts and one of those half tops with the back out that showed off her sexy abs. Working out is a big part of my life, so when I saw that Jas's body was tight, I was hooked.

I normally go to the Fraternal Order of Police Lodge on Thursdays because that's Motown night. Most cops, correctional officers and probation officers usually go on down, but now that more people have heard of it, it's definitely wall-to-wall with everybody. When Jas walked in, like most of the men in there, I instantly noticed her. Partly because she had the whole I-know-I'm-sexy-as-hell look about her and partly because I had never seen her in there before. I was on the dance floor getting my party on with this detective. I have to admit, I'm a danceaholic and I was making this chick look like an amateur. After we finished dancing, I went to the bathroom, and when I came out Jasmine was walking toward me. She gave me a wink and did this little trick with that damn tongue ring, and I was all hers. She asked me about my wedding band and I didn't lie about it. She said, "Perfect. No strings

BEWARE OF DOG!

attached." My sentiments exactly.

We started talking on the phone at first. Then, one night, I called off from work so that I could take Jas out to dinner. You see, I'll wine and dine the ladies in a heartbeat. Most men make the mistake of just wanting to hit it and don't expect to give out. I'm not so stupid to believe that anything in this life is free. So, I took Jas out to an all-night diner and we had some good food and some good laughter. I didn't expect anything to jump off that night. I drove her back to her place, expecting to maybe get a good-night kiss, the next thing I know she was grabbing my dick and I guess she was pleased with the findings. I'm just gon' put it out there, I only use plus-seven inch condoms. In case you've never heard of this, that's for the enlarged Mandingo Brotha. Now you know. Anyway, Jas grabbed the back of my neck and pulled me in for a kiss. She then told me to come with her. When we got up to her condo, she told me she wanted me to fuck her like never before. What's a man to do?

Sex with Jasmine is unlike anything that I've ever experienced before. Stacey is at minimum, okay in bed. Stacey used to be good, but after Ayanna was born she pretty much lost interest in sex—or at least it seems that way. Besides, after a while it gets old begging for some ass all of the time. Stacey's not down to try new and exciting things. Half of the time when I do approach her in an intimate way, she acts like I'm the last person in the world she wants to touch her. A man can only take so much. With Jas, it's different. She makes me feel like I'm the only man in the world for her. When we are getting horizontal, it's not just me doing all the foreplay. Jas is actually into it. The fact that she talks dirty to me when we're screwing is another turn-on for me. Now don't get me wrong, I love my wife and children and would never leave my family, but again,

4

BEWARE OF DOG!

what's a man to do? I saw this book written by Travis Hunter that caught my eye, Married But Still Looking, now that's me all the way.

See, the problem with Jas happened, when, like most women, she started wanting more. This is the part of women that I'll never understand. She was all cool at first. She knew about Stacey and the kids the night we met, and we've had many conversations about the fact that I love my wife and kids and I don't ever plan to go anywhere. Jas started whining about me not spending enough time with her and how I didn't call her enough. How fucked up is that?

So, I did the most logical thing any man with some sense would do—I took a step back. I didn't call her as much and I stopped going around her place as much too. Now that sounds sensible, right? Wrong! I should have just let Jas think that she was getting rid of me. There's nothing worse than a woman feeling pushed away, because that's exactly when she's going to attempt to pull you in even deeper. You, see, Miss Jas was not as down as I thought. She had my home phone number from day one. That Caller I.D. is the worse and will fuck up your game plan each and every time. Jas called Stacey and told her everything about us, even confirming the size and shape of my dick.

All men know that their mantra should be, "Baby, it wasn't me," but Stacey just wasn't having it. After all, this was my second time getting busted. Let me just tell you, Stacey ain't stupid for one minute, and I'm not so stupid to think that she doesn't know that I get my creep on. It's not something we talk about, but she sticks around for her own reasons. Maybe it's the kids or maybe she thinks that "men will be men," but whatever her reasons, it works for us.

About seven years ago, I was seeing this one girl and

BEWARE OF DOG!

she blew up my spot by visiting Stacey and telling her what was going on. Stacey and I argued, and I promised her that I'd change but it was just too hard. This time was different though. When Stacey found out that I was getting my groove on, yet again, she told me to leave. Like I said earlier, we've been together for so long that I used this opportunity to get in a little vacation. I rented a one-bedroom apartment from my aunt in Germantown and I laid it out real nice—you know, a man's bachelor's spot. I even made a little money on the side from a few of my boys. Whenever they wanted to lay low with a little shortie, I just charged them fifty dollars for the night, and the crib would officially be theirs. Half of the time I was chilling at one of my girls' house or I'd work a little overtime, so it all seemed to work out. I've never stopped loving my wife but we really did need a break. The only problem is that it was so hard, I mean really hard, to leave my kids. I got to see them on my days off and I would drive over in the afternoon to pick up Ayanna from day care and see my son home from school.

I knew Stacey was hurt, and my kids didn't understand why I no longer lived at home, but I just needed to clear my head. What did Stacey do next? Listening to her dumb-ass, jealous girlfriends, she went and filed for child support on a brotha. Next thing I know, I'm getting a court notice for a mediation hearing. One of my boys gave me a business card of a female attorney by the name of Troi Stokes, the most notorious family lawyer in Philadelphia. When I walked into her office, I nearly fell over. It was Troi, a woman that I had met a few years prior when I was giving a safe streets workshop at a Blacks In Government conference. We had spoken at the conference and had exchanged business cards and, of course, I was attracted to her, but not sexually. I had completely forgotten that I met her before our meeting.

BEWARE OF DOG!

Troi had always been fine. I remember the first time I saw her. It was the only time that I could recall being attracted to a woman's mind and not her body. Now don't get me wrong, Troi is and could always be a beauty queen. To put it mildly, she's fine! But when she introduced herself I was floored. She had all the qualities any man would want in a lady. I remember thinking that she was way too sophisticated for someone like me but I still wished that things were different. You see, back then, I wasn't nearly as wild as I am now. I was being true to Stacey. I knew then that there was no way Troi could represent me, you know, conflict of interest and everything but she gave me some really good advice. I tried taking her out to lunch but she told me her schedule was too hectic so we promised to stay in touch, but of course we never did. I guess she figured I was too much drama. Besides, it was better that way. Troi had always been silk and I'm just plain ole cotton. I took one look at her and wished that I could have turned back the hands of time. Troi was one of a kind.

The next day, I marched on down to family court with my receipts and what-not in tow, 'cause ain't nothing foolish about me. Well, the judge, who was a brotha—I mean brother, cause he wasn't no brotha of mine, sticks my ass for twelve hundred dollars a month in child support. Sell-out motherfucker.

There was absolutely no way I could afford to dress the way that I was accustomed, pay rent and my high-ass car note. Naw, I had to use my head and make a move, 'cause this dawg— had to get back in the house—and fast!

I called Stacey and told her I wanted to take her out for dinner. Shit, as much as I was paying in child support, her ass should have been taking me out. Anyway, I had to look at this like an investment. I took Stacey out to Ms. Tootsie's on South Street since that's one of her favorite soul food restaurants in

BEWARE OF DOG!

Philly. I thought we'd breeze on in, have some catfish, macaroni and cheese and some yams with their infamous watermelon iced tea. That should've been enough, but Stacey wanted to order dessert for not just us, but she even wanted to take some home to the kids. After that, she wanted to go to Zanzibar Blue to listen to some jazz music and get some drinks. Each time I calculated how much the evening was costing me I became more and more focused. I had to get my wife back. She was costing me a grip.

After our night out, I moved in for the final phase of the evening. I gave Stacey a little kiss on the lips and was about to turn around. I know Stacey like a book and I knew that she needed some good loving even if that meant me just holding her. No matter how bad things got between us, I knew she couldn't go too long without my plus seven, if you know what I mean? Stacey invited me in to my own house to talk. Now wasn't that some shit? Anyway, I know the best thing you can do for a woman is to communicate. So, I let Stacey open up to me, so she could tell me how she really felt. I promised her right then and there that I would never hurt her again. I had to say what I had to say to get back in, out from the dog's house.

The kids were at my mother-in-law's house for the night and that evening I romanced her and kissed her. By the time I pulled out the plus seven and laid down the good old Dexter stroke on her, just like that, I was back in. Well, at least for the moment. I wanted to play it right, not seem too eager—you know, make her think it was her idea that I came back home. As Stacey and I made love, she began crying hysterically and I gently kissed her tears away and even managed to cry with her. You know, Michael Baisden has a book out, Men Cry in the Dark and that shit is true. I told her over and over just how much I loved her and the kids and how important they all were

BEWARE OF DOG!

to me. Again, this wasn't a lie. I may be a lot of things, but I love my family, and no matter how many women I may meet, there ain't a damn one out there that can make me ever leave them. Never!

I spent the next day with Stacey and the kids, and we went to one of those indoor fun zone places. It felt so good to spend time with my family, something that I hadn't done in so long. That night, Stacey asked me to move back in, permanently. Within two weeks I had let all of my side honeys go and I made a clean break.

Now, don't get me wrong, I let my side honeys go for a variety of reasons. First, all three of them were all wrong for me. I hate to admit this, but one of my old heads schooled me about how to be a true player. I have a coworker, Rodney Ulman. He's a retired police officer and I look up to him for a variety of reasons. One night, before Rodney retired, we were working and Rodney was telling me about his own situation. You see, Rodney has been married to the same woman for thirty years. He met his wife when he was a junior in college and she was a young, seventeen-year-old freshman. Rodney attended Morehouse and his wife, Alicia, was attending Spelman College. Anyway, Rodney was telling me that I had no idea how to be a successfully married man. I have to admit that at first, I was taken aback at his comments. Who the hell did he think he was? So, I listened to the old head, because hell, you never know when you can incorporate something new in your life and build upon it. So, Rodney was telling me that he was happily married to his wife, but he was also quite content with his full-time girlfriend that he's been seeing for ten years and his two part-time girlfriends. Now, I was truly shocked.

"Where in the hell can you find so much time to spend with all of these women?" I asked.

BEWARE OF DOG!

"You see, young playa, you don't need a whole lot of time. My first rule of thumb is to take care of home, first and foremost. I've been married for thirty years and I'll be married for thirty more, God willing. I would never leave my wife. Now, each of my women, with the exception of my full-time girlfriend are all happily married. My full timer was married, but she's been divorced for the past three years. That is causing me some grief because now she's beginning to want more. So, as much as I love her, I may have to cut her off soon, because she's now becoming a liability," Rodney explained.

"Well then tell me how the hell a man your age, and I mean no disrespect, has enough energy to keep up with three extra women," I asked.

"Women my age don't need a whole lot of time. The women I'm involved with know my situation and I know theirs. If I can spend an hour or two with them at lunch time, I'm a happy man and so are they. I make it a rule that my extra women must be happily married or seriously involved with someone and that they be at least more than forty years old. You couldn't pay me to creep with some young tender thang. You better get hip youngblood," Rodney warned.

I thought about my own situation and they were all single. If I were going to be back with my family, I had a few new rules for my new and improved ways. Now, don't get all bent out of shape, but I'm going to get my creep on, you can best believe that. I just have a few cardinal rules now that so that I don't ever end up in my previous predicament.

Rule number one: Never—and I do mean never—mess around with a woman who's not married. This rule can save your life. Remember that side honey, Jasmine? See, she's the perfect example. Single, no kids, good job and no man. She

BEWARE OF DOG!

had way too much time to devote to married ole me. Had she been married, then she would have been spending all of that extra time with her husband and her own damn family. Single women with no kids are dangerous. I don't care how much single women tell you that all they're looking for is a married man because they're on the professional career move and they don't have time for a committed relationship. Don't believe them! If you don't believe me, just read about Kobe Bryant and Reverend Jesse Jackson's relationship woes. Shall I go on? This leads me to my next rule.

Rule number two: never, never, never...Did I say never? Don't have sex without protection and make sure you bring backups. Preferably condoms. They reduce the risk of STDs, unwanted pregnancy and AIDS. I know you've heard horror stores about women using turkey basters to extract semen from themselves after sex and women inserting small holes in the condom to get a man all caught up. You'd be surprised how many scandalous women are out there who are just desperate to have a baby. The final result is your marriage is all jacked up and you're paying all sorts of child-support payments and the list goes on and on.

Rule number three: Never call your side honey from your house. Caller I.D. and *69 were probably invented by a playa hater. I made that mistake with Jas. Here I was calling her from home when Stacey wasn't there so Jas had my telephone number. Of course she never told me, but hey, I guess that was a part of her master plan. Matter of fact, don't even tell the side honey what part of the city you live in. If you live in Pennsylvania, tell her you live in New Jersey. Next thing you know, the side honey is driving around your neighborhood looking for your car and asking folks if they know you and what-not.

BEWARE OF DOG!

Rule number four: I know this one is a stretch, but for my fellas out there, try thinking like a woman. You see, a man will get caught cheating each and every time. You know a lot of women get so many ideas about the cheating game from those books they read. You know the average man watches sports, scratches his balls and farts around the house fixing shit. If you notice, the average woman always has her nose stuck in a damn book. Us men need to start reading the same books women are reading. We need to stay up on our game. We need to face the facts. We just don't know how to do it. Eddie Murphy said it best, "Men are like dogs and women are like cats." You let a dog out the gate and he just starts running, doesn't even know where he's going, but he's going. You let a cat out the door, and she starts looking around first, all cautious and then that cat will sashay off into the night, next thing you know it's daylight and the cat just sashays on back in and you wonder, now where in the hell have you been? The cat just licks her paws and says, "meow." We need to listen to women and see how it should be done. That's why I will never mess around with a side honey past three months. After that, feelings can begin to grow at a rapid speed, and the next thing you know, you actually start to care about her and start getting jealous when she tells you she's going out with her girlfriends, while you go on about your business with your own damn family. If at all possible, start acting like an asshole and if you're lucky, she'll break it off with you. If she's mad, she won't want to talk to you and you never have to worry about her tracking you down and trying to spoil your shit.

Rule number five: If all else fails and you get caught, don't ever admit to anything. Even if you're in mid-pump— deny it forever.

So, that's my story. I have my rules in place, I have my

BEWARE OF DOG!

side honey at the moment. She's married to some investment broker and they have a son. Her husband is always on the road, probably doing his own damn thing. We spend a few times a month together and it's all good. It ain't no cause to be greedy, you know? My partner, Clinton, I like to call him Zen Buddha because he thinks he's a damn saint. You know the type, eats live and sleeps church—always trying to school me and tell me how I should be living. We're the same age and he's been married to his wife, Teresa, for ten years. They have three boys and Clinton acts as if he's never cheated on his wife, but come on I know the real deal. We always have these philosophical conversations while we're in the police cruiser. Last week, I couldn't take it anymore, so I just asked him the obvious.

"Man, you've never, ever thought about cheating on your wife?" I asked.

"I see booty everywhere I turn. Fidelity and my integrity are important to me. If I don't have either one those, I've got nothing. Fidelity: don't let the actions of the man diminish the value of the word," Clinton replied.

"Man, you can talk all that Zen Buddha shit all you want, but don't tell me that you don't at least dream about getting with another woman. Every man does."

"You're a straight nut, man. You have a wonderful wife and two great children. I can't see why people risk all they've built on a cheap thrill. Besides that, you took vows. You need to learn to honor them. "

" 'Cause, man, there's only one thing better than pussy, and that's some new pussy."

"Let me ask you this: Do you even use protection when you sleep with these knuckle-heads?" Clinton asked.

"Hell yeah. I'd be crazy not to. I see I'm goin' have to

13

share my golden rules with you, man."

"Please don't," he replied.

"Man, you just don't get it. I just can't see being with the same woman forever. I have the best of both worlds. I love Stacey and always will. We have a great relationship, but being with the same woman is like an unsharpened pencil—there's no point."

"I see you're in rare form today. What? You got a book of clichés in your back pocket?" Clinton asked. "How would you feel if you found out Stacey was stepping out on you?"

"In the words of Cedric the Entertainer, 'I wish a nucca would,' " I responded.

"Big Mama said it best, 'A hard head makes a soft behind.' I see you're going to have to learn the hard way. If you should ever decide to join us, I recently started a men's fellowship ministry. Why don't you come out and learn how to apply a few values and morals to your marriage."

"Man, don't start with all of that J.J. crap. I ain't trying to hear it."

"J.J.? What's that?"

"Man, you don't know? Everybody refers to you as Jesus Junior because you're always preaching."

"I've been called many names in my life, and trust me when I tell you, that's an honor you should aspire to be called as well."

"Beat it, man. Stop preaching. We've got work to do."

I was a political science major at Temple University in Philadelphia and Clinton majored in criminology at Florida A&M University. Clinton is always trying to persuade me to be faithful but I'm my own man. I stand alone. Just because I have a little variety outside of my marriage doesn't make me a bad person. Like I said in the beginning, I love my wife and kids and I wouldn't trade them for all of the tea in China. I've got this thing under control. What could possibly go wrong? Right?

"Ashes fly back into the face of he who throws them."
—African proverb

Chapter 2

Stacey

If the saying, you fool me once shame on you, fool me twice shame on me is true, then I should just be ashamed of myself for all of eternity. Men will never learn. I've been married for twelve long years, and I've seen a lot of bullshit in my day. I got married when I was only twenty-one. I met Xavier while I was attending Temple University. I had high hopes back then. You couldn't tell me I wasn't going to be the next well-known news anchor in Philadelphia. To pay for school I had a few modeling jobs, and I even appeared in a few commercials. The money was good, but the exposure to the industry was even better. I met a few people in the business, and I was lining myself up for my bright and shiny future.

I met Xavier just after high school. He has always been a true ladies' man, with his dark skin, his jet-black, curly hair and his six-four muscular frame. The first time I saw him playing basketball was during my freshman year. Xay was a sophomore. I knew that I had to have him. The only problem is that three other women felt the same way, but I wasn't about being one of his groupies. Sure, I thought he was attractive but

BEWARE OF DOG!

my mama is from Meridian, Mississippi, and she taught me how to be a southern belle—let the man chase you.

Anyway, I guess my Southern charm worked because the more I ignored Xavier, the more he became persistent. Of course his little fan club was hating me left and right but you think I cared? I've never really been liked by a bunch of females anyway. Back then I was really naïve but then hindsight is always twenty-twenty. After two years of dating, during my junior year in college, I got pregnant so I had to drop out of school. I was devastated and saw my whole future come crashing down before me. Xavier's father is a minister in Philadelphia, and he convinced his son to do the honorable thing. We had a small wedding at my father-in-law's church and the rest as they say is history.

My parents attended and it seemed that my mother cried each time she saw me carrying around that big belly. One day I asked her why she was always crying and she told me that she wanted more for me and didn't want me to have the same life she had lived all of those years. My dad had been cheating on my mom since even before they got married. My mother knew about my father's infidelity, but my parents have four children together. My mother's question to me was, "Where am I going?" My sister and I would always try to convince my mom to stand up for herself. I vowed that I wouldn't be that type of wife. So after Xavier and I got married, I promised myself that I would be the best damn wife known to man so that he'd have no excuse to want another woman.

I worked in a bank for the first five years of our marriage and to be honest, Xavier was good to me and good for me. Xay has always wanted to be a federal agent, but after graduation he took the federal exams, all of them, too, but it just never worked out. Xay took the police department's exam and

was offered an appointment to the police academy just four months later. I was so proud of my baby, but I was scared to death for his safety. But I wanted to be a supportive wife, so I never told him of my fears. Every time he walked out that door, I made sure we weren't upset with each other and I made sure I said a little prayer before he left. I'd let God do the rest.

I cooked, cleaned and sexed my man whenever he wanted and even times when I didn't, but I then realized that things just weren't the same. I chalked it up to being married to the same person for so long that you just begin to get bored, because Lord knows I lost my sex drive, fast. Then one day, a girl came in the bank and asked me if I knew a guy named Xavier. I told her that he was my husband and she told me they had been together, intimately, a few times and she had even been in my house. Apparently, Xavier told her that I was his sister and Justin was his nephew. I was so upset that I told my manager that I had to get the hell out of there. I went straight to my mama's house and I attempted to cry on her shoulder, but she turned her back on me. Her exact words were: "Honey, get used to it. This is exactly why I wanted you to get your education so that you would never have to depend on some man for the type of life you've become accustomed to living. Now, I suggest you handle your business."

"What do you mean, handle my business?" I questioned.

"Get your financial affairs in order so that if he decides to walk off and leave, you have all of your ducks in a row. Don't end up like me. Look at me. I'm stuck, and I don't have anything to do but wait for your daddy to close his eyes for good or simply put up with this shit," Mama responded.

"What am I going to do? I have to leave him. I can't stay with some man who cheats on me," I tried to explain.

BEWARE OF DOG!

"Well then you don't want a man. Because I ain't never met a man out there, alive or dead, who doesn't cheat. You got your reverends and your average men, but find me one and I'll mold him for all of us women. You leave your husband and that'll be the biggest mistake you've ever made. You meet and marry another one and I promise you he'll do the same damn thing, and you meet and marry the next one after that and it'll just keep on repeating itself. Just be happy you got a man who has all of his teeth, a good job, doesn't hit on you and I'd say that you've hit the jackpot. But you can do what you like. That's just my opinion," Mama said sadly.

My father died a year later of a heart attack and my mother was devastated. The funeral was especially hard for me, because I really loved my daddy. Don't you know three days after we buried my daddy, a girl that I had seen in my neighborhood visited my parents' house and introduced herself as my sister. Apparently, my dad had fathered this girl who was three years younger than me and who is six months older than my younger brother. She even had the birth certificate to prove it.

Anyway, a week after I learned of Xay's first bout with infidelity, I enrolled in night classes at Temple University to get my degree. I had to line all my ducks in a row, just the way Mama warned. Xay had the degree, not me. I completed my degree and finally decided it might be time to have another child, but then Xay started his damn creeping again and there was no way that I was going to bring another child into the world like that. So, I continued to work hard and finally, after many long days when I just wanted to hurl myself in front of the proverbial train, I finally saw the light at the end of the tunnel and I finished school. I then set out to change my life. My marriage was a joke. It doesn't take a rocket scientist to tell

BEWARE OF DOG!

me that. I had come up with a few rules for myself.

Rule number one: Make sure that you're financially straight. If you finally decide that you've had enough, make sure you can continue to live the way you're accustomed to living without that man's help. Too many of us put up with the bullshit because we have to. Two years ago, I finally decided it was now or never and so my beautiful little angel, Ayanna, was born. You'd think Xavier would have ceased his nonsense, but oh no. It just got a little worse. Although Xavier and I have our problems, our children are just about the best thing we've got going for our marriage. Surprisingly, even with all of our troubles, it's not all that bad. After I began working for the police department, I figured it would be a good way to keep my eye on Xay, but then I had the accident and so now I'm on to plan B.

Rule number two: If you catch your man and the other woman in the act don't go all buck wild on the woman—unless you know her. The woman may be just as in the dark as you. Don't risk going to jail over some dumb crap.

Rule number three: If you know the woman, kick her ass! This is necessary because she knew that you were married and still decided to sleep with your husband. Matter of fact, kick both of their asses.

Rule number four: Either way, make a decision and stick to it. Big Mama used to always say, "If you lie than you'll steal, if you'll steal than you'll cheat." In other words, If you're capable of doing it once, you're capable of doing it twice. If you're going to move on then move on. Don't keep taking that cheating-ass man back. Make him piss on the pot or get off. Hell, we all know only fools gamble twice!

Rule number five: If you can't beat them, join them. Don't be no fool, but make them think you're just about the

BEWARE OF DOG!

most gullible thing known to man. Cover your tracks and make sure you protect yourself. Always stay one step ahead of the man.

Rule number six: If all else fails, just pray!

I will tell you this, I was faithful to my husband for all of my marriage. I listened to my mother so intently that she had me actually believing that there were no good men out there, but I'm here to tell you that it's just not the case. I have so many male friends that let me know how some men really are and truth be told you have scandalous men and women.

I recently met the love of my life. Captain Chris Willis is my supervisor, and we recently hooked up after many long talks and after being led into a world I thought I'd never even known existed. I have never known ecstasy like this before. Damn! I still haven't realized if it's the sex or the intimacy that made me even give Chris the time of day. I will admit that the power my baby commands is so very attractive.

I guess I'll never really know what made me make the decision to enter into this world of deceit, lies and unfamiliarity. The worse types of extramarital affairs are the ones that begin with the emotions. It's a shame that Xay wouldn't know how to get in touch with my emotions if I drew him a road map.

Now, I know that I shouldn't shit where I eat, but hey, it just sort of happened. If you are going to play where they pay then you'd better be smart enough to climb high up the chain of command. Chris is so good to me because my baby was the one who got me promoted downtown. Now, that's not to say that I didn't have the right kind of qualifications, but hell, it doesn't hurt to have a little push from time to time. My sweetie is a little older than me, but sometimes the more seasoned folks know how to treat a lady. Xavier doesn't have a damn clue! He couldn't buy a piece of pussy from me with a golden dollar bill.

BEWARE OF DOG!

I know he's out there creepin' yet again, but I could care less.

Last year, I got a hold of my credit report, and I worked hard to pay off these damn high-interest credit cards we have. I even paid Xavier's shit off too. I don't want no excuses this time for him not being able to pay his damn child support payments because I've already done the research and he's going to have to pay at least fifteen hundred dollars a month on his salary. I have about another month of this tired-ass bullshit and then I'm out for good and I ain't looking back. Quiet as it's kept, I have a three-bedroom house located in Chestnut Hill that I'm closing on in about two months. Chris has been so supportive, helping me to get my life back on track. Once I'm out this house, it's going to be on and popping. I don't have time for the drama anymore. My new life with her is going to be everything that I could ever imagine and more. I mean it's true. Women are definitely better lovers than men, right?

"A fool may chance to put something into a wise man's head."
—African proverb

Chapter 3

Troi

As my personal telephone line in my office rang for the third time in five minutes, I threw my hand over my forehead. It was more than likely my best friend, Corie Simms, calling for the umpteenth time that afternoon. Corie was trying desperately to get me to come to her club, The Blue Nile, after work and meet her for a drink. I really needed to finish reviewing the report that my paralegal, Debra Frink, had been working on so diligently for the past six months. If all went well, my law firm, Stokes and Associates, would be taking its reputation to the next level because I was looking to add on two new partners. The only problem, like always, I was trying to be everything to everybody, you know, pulling myself in a million different directions. I had so much to do before my much-anticipated business trip to New York City in only two days. Before the voice mail picked up, I snatched the receiver from its cradle.

"Troi Stokes speaking. How may I help you?" I announced in my professional business tone.

"Hey, girl. I just called to remind you of a few things

23

BEWARE OF DOG!

before you make a dash for the door."

It was Jennifer Blackson, one of my counterparts from Virginia.

"Hey yourself. What is it now? I swear I've spoken to you more times this week than I have all year, " I said, knowing exactly why Jennifer was calling, yet again.

Jennifer is a cool-ass white girl and a bona fide party animal, nothing more and nothing less. She recently told me that after a lifetime of battling the bulge, she had finally lost 110 pounds and looked fantastic. I couldn't wait to see her since she lived in Fredericksburg, Virginia. The last we had seen each other was in Las Vegas, about six months ago in December and she was on her way then. Sadly, Jennifer's husband still thought she had a fat butt. You know most white guys think that way about white women, but the brothas were hollering at Jennifer left and right.

"I need you to do me a huge favor," Jennifer said in her thick southern drawl.

"What is it, girl? You know I gotta get home and spend some quality time with my fiancé before New York and I still haven't finished this damn report," I said.

"I need for you to do a presentation on child custody issues. I had someone else lined up from my office who was supposed to do it, but that fell through. Please?" Jennifer begged.

"Aw damn, that's just what I need, more stress added to my day. Where am I supposed to find time to put together a presentation? This is such short notice," I said.

"Don't worry. I'll bring my laptop and put together an outline for you while I'm on the train. You won't have to present until sometime later in the week, so we'll have plenty of time for you to make any revisions," Jennifer explained.

BEWARE OF DOG!

"Fine. You're lucky this is what I do for a living," I responded as I cleared my desk.

After graduating from Mount Holyoke College in Massachusetts, I attended Harvard Law School and obtained my law degree in 1998. Since I graduated at the top of my class, I was hired by a major law firm in downtown Philadelphia. I've always wanted to start my own law firm, so two years ago, when the opportunity presented itself, I opened a small family law firm with just me and my paralegal, Debra. Now, two years later, I'm proud to say that I have a team of six lawyers and two additional paralegals. My dream is to basically run the entire legal system in Philly, but like my mama always says, you've got to crawl before you can walk.

"See, I knew I could count on you. I owe you big time. Now, what I really called you for is to ask what you're packing for the trip. Make sure you pack extra after-work outfits, because I wanna get my party on, girl," Jennifer said.

I used to get my swerve on back in my college days and even for a while before I became engaged. Actually, the fact that I've been engaged now for more than three years really hasn't stopped a thing. I just like partying in more professional atmospheres and usually with my fiancé. We often meet for his after-work affairs or mine.

I became involved with Malcolm Cooke at a fairly young age. I was just a mere twenty-five years old when we became engaged and I just knew that I had seen enough of the world and all that it had to offer. Malcolm and I are the same age, and I met him while visiting my best friend, Corie, at Fisk University in 1990. Malcolm and I began dating and became engaged in 2000. He actually proposed to me on New Year's Eve on the steps of the Art Museum in Philadelphia. He's the love of my life. We have the picture-perfect relationship, we're

BEWARE
OF
DOG!

a D.I.N.K. couple—double income, no kids. I like it just that
way. With my business practice sending me all over the country
on various business trips, who has time to raise a family? I was
in Phoenix in February, Chicago in March, Denver in April and
Seattle in May and now off to New York City on Sunday.
That's why it's so important that I have a nice quality weekend
with my man. I mean traveling is nice, but I miss sleeping in
my king-size bed with my man. Malcolm is actually the best
thing that has ever happened to me. We both cook, clean and he
is definitely a B.M.W. (Black Man Working). I mean the man
works too hard sometimes. Malcolm owns his own record label
in Center City Philadelphia and he's also the business partner of
my best friend Corie. He's a really a good man. Don't get me
wrong, we've had our share of trouble in the past, but he's a
pretty good man.

    "All right, girl, slow your roll. I'll pack some hoochie
wear, but don't think you're going to keep me out all night, until
the wee hours of the morning. I need my beauty rest, and I
want to use this trip as sort of a relaxation getaway," I said.

    "Girl, save it. How often do we get to travel together?
Just make sure you call me the minute you get to the hotel. I'll
be waiting. Oh yeah, don't forget to call Dee when you get
there. She wants us to come to her place and have dinner or
something like that," Jennifer reminded me.

    "I mean I'm excited to see my girl, too, but I'd rather go
out to dinner, I mean we are on somewhat of a getaway trip.
You know what I'm sayin'? Besides, I wanna see the town. I
don't have time to be sitting up in some hot-ass loft in Brooklyn
all night long. I wanna be out," I exclaimed.

    "I know, me too," Jennifer agreed.

    "All right, well let me get off this phone so I can get this
work done and over with. I'll see you in the Big Apple. Be

BEWARE
OF
DOG!

careful and have a safe trip up there," I said to Jennifer.

"Same here. I'll check with you later. Bye now," Jennifer responded in that southern drawl.

After I checked and rechecked the entire case file and everything was on point, I cleaned off my desk and prepared to leave for the rest of the week. I was really looking forward to being out of the office for one solid week. I checked with Debra and gave her instructions on everything that I would need for her to basically run the office while I was out. Let's keep it real, she's the one who really makes things happen. I have mad trust for her. I said my good-byes and was off to be with my baby.

Malcolm and I own a large brownstone on Twenty-second and Spruce Streets. When I told Corie that Malcolm and I were purchasing our home before the wedding she tried to talk me out of it, but in only six months, on New Year's Eve, Malcolm and I would be married, at the Art Museum, nonetheless!

I love the downtown area. I love the city and wouldn't trade it for any day of the week. Most of our friends live in the suburbs of New Jersey and Delaware, but I simply love downtown Philly. It has so much to offer and besides, my office is only minutes from home. Most of the time I walk to work instead of fighting city traffic. Since the weather was so hot and humid, I took off my silk jacket, put on my sneakers and walked the ten minutes home. I figured that I would get there and make a nice, quiet dinner, just the two of us.

When I arrived home, I was pleasantly surprised that Malcolm had cleaned up the entire house, and although it was daylight, the place was covered with peach-scented candles and there was a huge bouquet of yellow, red, peach and white roses on the large oak table in the foyer. Although I had a huge salad

27

BEWARE OF DOG!

at lunch, I was starving and the aroma of Italian food, my favorite, permeated the air.

As I stepped inside, there were various colors of rose petals covering the floor. On the table where I normally set my keys was a note card that read: This weekend is all about us. I love you. Go to the stairs and you'll find another note. I followed the order and traveled to the staircase. The second note read: Remove all of your clothing and then go to the top of the stairs. Again, I did as I was ordered. When I reached the top of the stairs, there was another card and this one said: Follow the rose petals. The rose petals led me to our master bathroom, which was filled with more candles, all kinds of flowers and my favorite Javier CD playing. I climbed in the tub and as I lay my head back and closed my eyes, I forgot all about the problems that Malcolm and I had in the past and just wanted to savor the moment that I wished could last forever.

"I see you know how to follow directions." Malcolm's deep voice penetrated the air. I looked up to find him stark naked, which was a treat in itself.

"Hi, baby. This is wonderful. Just what the doctor ordered."

"So you like? See, I know how to be romantic."

"I definitely like. Come here and let me show you just how much."

Malcolm walked over and climbed in back of me into the huge whirlpool. He gently massaged my temples then my shoulders before moving his huge hands around to my medium-sized breasts. He slid his hands down to my thighs and slid open the mouth of my vagina. I let out a soft moan, and Malcolm knew that he had all of me.

We must have stayed in bed for about two hours. By the time we got around to dinner the lasagna was cold and the salad

BEWARE OF DOG!

was wilted, but I didn't mind one bit. We stayed in the house that night and made love over and over. Times like this reminded me why I wanted to get married so badly.

I had been dating Malcolm off and on since I had met him while we were both in college. When I graduated from law school we began to date seriously. After three years, I had felt that enough was enough. Either Malcolm was going to make an honest woman out of me, or it was over. Yeah, I gave him a little push. Well all right, I gave him a damn ultimatum, but sometimes women have to do these kinds of things. About two years ago, right before Malcolm proposed, things began to get a little shaky. I guess you could say that I'm from the old school and although I love my man, there are just some things that I'm not down with. Malcolm is a little too freaky for me. On two occasions, Malcolm has brought women home with him and subtly suggested that we have a ménage a trois. He tried to play things off, saying that the woman he came home with was one of his singers and he needed to find some papers for her to sign, but I knew better. I saw the hungry look she had in her eyes and after I gave her one of those sista-girl stares, she and Malcolm backed off. Since he never came outright and said this was why he brought her home, I dropped the subject.

Malcolm is also into anal sex and I just can't, nor I won't get with that. I don't know where this fetish has come from, but I'm just not down with that. I hear so many of my female friends say that they're down with that, but to me, if a man likes anal sex, it just sends a red flag up that he may be bisexual. My theory is all anuses were created equal. Malcolm insists that my butt is so much different from a man's and that he's not attracted to men, but we've had major arguments about this. Why doesn't he let me stick something up his ass? This ass is for exit only! Anyway, one would think we have major

29

BEWARE OF DOG!

issues, but that is pretty much the extent of things that are placing a burden on our relationship.

My weekend of romance ended too soon. Before I knew it, it was Sunday morning and I wasn't even packed. Malcolm was downstairs in his office, and I began the tedious job of sorting out my clothes for my trip. Whenever I travel I always have way too many items, but a girl has to have options. I hate getting caught without the right thing to wear and then having to scramble around looking for an outfit. I'm always prepared— from swimming to evening wear, I'm ready.

The phone rang and I contemplated answering it. I looked at the Caller I.D. and noticed it was Corie. I snatched the phone from the receiver.

"What the fuck do you want?"

"Hi, little boy. Whatcha doing?" Corie asked, ignoring my rudeness.

"Packing."

"Oh yeah, I forgot you were leaving me. Where are you going again?"

"For the tenth time, I'm going to New York."

"And how long did you say you'd be gone?"

"Like always, until Friday. Don't you ever listen to me?"

"Uh, not really. I try not to."

"Fuck you," I responded.

"I just may have to visit you up there. I'm due for a vacation," Corie said.

"Let me know. The hotel that I'm staying in is the bomb. I have a two-bedroom suite reserved."

"Why do you need so much space?"

"Uh, because I'm a princess?" I responded.

"Try again, sweetie."

30

BEWARE OF DOG!

"No, in case Dee wants to spend the night or something. I just like the extra space. Plus, it's a business write-off. Who cares?"

"I'm going to have to get back with you on that. I just may shoot up there," Corie replied.

"All right let me know. I'll call you when I get there and give you the number."

"Okie dokie. I don't want to talk to you anymore, little boy. Peace out," Corie said as she hung up the phone in my ear.

Corie is the only person in this world who can speak to me the way she does and not catch a beat down and vice versa. It would take Corie to call me little boy, since she's always trying so hard to be different and calling me a boy is truly different. Malcolm tried to play me out one time and speak to me the way Corie did and he caught a straight up and down cuss whooping.

Corie and I have been friends since birth. Our parents have been long-time friends since they knew each other while living in Guyana. We're both only children, and we've become closer than any two sisters ever could.

After packing, I realized it was still early and since I had three hours before I had to be to Thirtieth Street station, I figured I'd get me a little afternoon nookie. I dragged my two suitcases downstairs and left them in the foyer. Malcolm was working on his keyboard, in the den, which was converted into a small studio. I decided I would have a little replay of Friday and Saturday. I quickly removed all of my clothing and stood in front of the keyboard. He didn't bother to look up so I cleared my throat.

"What's up, babe?"

"You have to ask?"

"I'm kind of busy. I've been working on this tune all

31

day and I can't seem to get it to sound the way I want it to. What's up?" Malcolm asked shortly.

"Again, do you have to ask? I just figured that since I'm going to be away all week and after you drop me off you have the rest of the day to work on music stuff, we could play a little."

"Baby, not right now. I'm not in the mood," Malcolm stated as he placed his reading glasses back on and kept punching on the keyboard.

"Sweetie, by the time I get back, my period will be on and you know how horny I've been lately." Nothing, he said absolutely nothing. He just kept ignoring a sista.

I swiped the music sheets to the floor and began climbing on his lap.

"What the fuck did you do that for? I told you I was busy. Can't you take a fucking hint?" he exploded.

"Wait a minute, I'm trying to be romantic with my damn fiancé and he's treating me like a fucking flea."

"Damn, I give you the whole fucking weekend and that's not good enough. I give you a fucking inch and you want a whole motherfucking yard!" he continued.

"I don't believe this shit. You always find a damn way to blame everything on me. Here I'm trying to spend some quality fucking time with dumb-ass fiancé and he's too busy to do me!"

"Fuck you!" he responded.

"No, fuck you!" I replied as I picked up my dress and ran out the studio. I made sure that I slammed the door so hard I'm sure it broke. I got dressed, grabbed my luggage and headed out the door.

As I pulled out of the garage, I couldn't believe this shit was happening on the day that I was leaving. I hated going away on terms like this, but after the way he treated me, I was

BEWARE OF DOG!

damn sure not calling him before I boarded that train.

I pulled out my cell phone and called Corie.

"I'm on my way over."

"What's wrong?"

"I hate that asshole!"

Corie lives just five blocks from us. She also has a downtown brownstone and that just makes my life so much easier. When I pulled up Corie had the garage door open and I pulled into her second port. I forgot her C class Mercedes was in the shop.

"I'm going to need a ride to the train station," I stated as I walked up the stairs from the garage and noticed Corie standing in the doorway.

"You wanna talk about it?" she asked.

"Fuck him. He's a bastard from hell, and I can't stand his fucking guts."

"Okay, tell me how you really feel. I get the feeling that you're holding back how you really feel."

"Fuck you," I said, laughing at Corie's sarcasm.

Just then, Corie's friend Rashan came out of the bathroom. He gave me one of those thuggish nods and whispered something in Corie's ear then walked out the front door. I can't stand him—actually rarely do I like any of Corie's boyfriends. She only dates the thug type and guys who are married. It was something about this Rashan, though, that really rubbed me the wrong way.

"I didn't know you had company. You should have told me."

"And done what? You know that every nail that's attached to this house belongs to me. All of this is my shit. I wanted him to leave anyway. His time with me has expired anyway. He's starting to catch feelings and shit, and you know

BEWARE OF DOG!

I can't have that."

I told Corie what happened and as usual she tried to stay neutral—well at least for a few minutes she gave it a shot.

"I think you should call him before I take you to the train. Don't go away mad at your fiancé, especially going to New York of all places."

"Fuck him."

"Fuck 'im then," Corie responded.

Corie took me to the train and I promised that I would call her the minute I arrived and settled in to my hotel. The ride was smooth, and before I knew it I was pulling into Penn Station. I love New York. The last time I was there was, seven months ago, in November and it was pretty damn cold so I was really looking forward to spending summer in the city. Ain't nothing like New York City. I was staying at the South Gate Towers Hotel, which was directly across from Penn Station, so I didn't have to worry about a taxi or anything. I checked in, retrieved my messages from the front desk and traveled to the twenty-third floor to my room.

After I unpacked, I called Corie and gave her my room and phone numbers. We talked for a few minutes then I decided to call my idiot fiancé and let him know that I had arrived safely.

"Hello," he answered dryly.

"Hey, I just called to let you know I got here safely and to give you the phone number.

"What's the number?" he asked even more dryly.

"It's 212-555-7546."

"All right."

"All right," I responded

"Bye."

I didn't even say good-bye I just hung up in his damn

ear. He didn't even warrant me saying good bye.

Jennifer had left me a message at the front desk, informing me to call her when I settled in.

"I'm here." I yelled into the phone when she picked up.

"Wonderful. Are you all unpacked?" she asked.

"Yeah. What's on the itinerary?"

"Well, I checked out the hotel sports bar, and it's jumping. I haven't eaten yet. Do you wanna meet down there for some dinner?"

"Sounds like a plan to me. I'll meet you there in ten minutes," I said.

I jumped in the shower and changed into another sundress. I love cute little sundresses and that's all I practically wear in the summertime. I checked myself in the mirror and noticed how good I was looking lately. Working out had really given my otherwise scrawny frame a little meat to it. I had the whole Halle Berry look going for myself—at least that's what I saw in the mirror. I walked into the hallway and as I did I noticed a tall, dark—and I do mean dark—milk chocolate, fine brotha man walking toward me with three bags of luggage. The guy's shoulder bag fell, and I bent down to pick it up for him.

"Do you need some help with these?" I offered

"No thanks. I can manage," Milk responded, displaying the most evenly white brights I'd ever seen.

"Suit yourself."

I kept walking and put a little bounce to my step. I'd been taking this basic training class at my fitness center and I knew that my booty was straight on point. By the time I reached the elevator, I pressed the button and it opened immediately. Before I stepped on, I turned to my right and Milk was checking me out. I gave him one of my own white-bright smiles and got my flirting self on the elevator.

BEWARE OF DOG!

When I stepped off, I couldn't help but notice how many men of all shapes, sizes, colors and ages were in the lobby. Jennifer was in the sports bar and true to her word, she looked fantastic. She had lost the weight and had the great looks to go along with it.

"Girl, did you see all the men in this hotel?" Jennifer asked. "Yeah, and I just ran into one of the finest on my floor. What's up with that?"

"There's an in-service being held here. These guys are from Morgan Stanley. They'll be here for three weeks."

"That explains why that guy had so much luggage. He must be here for that seminar."

"Honey, I'm here to have some fun. I left my jackass husband home and the kids are at their grandparents' for the rest of the summer and I intend to have a little fun while I'm here this week."

"I heard that," I added, thinking Jennifer and I had a lot in common in the jackass man department.

Jennifer and I were having so much fun getting to know all the guys from the investment firm. They were buying drinks, and we were flashing smiles all over the house. Three guys from the firm asked if they could sit with us, and it was all good until the black guy tried to push up on me—all four feet of him. He told me that he hated women who smoked, so I excused myself so I could go and buy me a pack of cigarettes. I don't smoke, but if that was going to give brotha man the hint, I was willing to try anything.

As I squeezed through the crowded bar and tried to make my way to the front, I felt someone grab my hand.

"Are you going to just walk past me and not introduce yourself?" Milk asked.

"Oh, I see you settled in. I tried to offer you a helping

BEWARE OF DOG!

hand earlier but you rejected my assistance."

"I was trying to be a gentleman. I didn't want you to wrinkle up that pretty little dress you have on," Milk said as he looked me slowly up and down. For a minute I thought he was the Bionic Man, because you couldn't tell me that he wasn't seeing straight through my clothes.

"I'm Gavin Thompkins. How do you do?" he said as he extended his strong hand toward me.

"That's a different name. What does your name mean?" I asked.

"I really don't know."

"I see. Well, I'm Troi Stokes," I said as he accepted my hand and turned it over.

"I see your husband really loves you," Milk stated as he admired the ice on my ring finger.

"It's my fiancé and I see your wife truly cares about you," I said as I turned his left hand over and admired his platinum wedding band.

"I love your sense of humor. Are you always this funny?"

"I've been told a time or two that I'm a little silly."

"I love your accent. Where are you from?"

"I'm from Philly, and I don't think I've ever been told I have an accent."

"I'm from Baltimore. I guess just right up the road from Philly. How long are you going to be staying here, Troi?"

"I'll be here all week. I leave on Friday."

"Before you leave, perhaps I can convince you to have dinner with me."

"We'll see."

"I'm not a killer. I promise," Gavin said as he flashed that smile at me again. For some reason, that did it. This man

BEWARE OF DOG!

may have not been a killer, but he damn sure was dangerous for me. He was just too attractive, and I wasn't about to start nothing I had no intention of finishing.

Although Malcolm was being an asshole, we were destined to be married. For better or for worse. I'm going to take my wedding vows seriously and there was no way that I was going to risk my future marriage over some stupid crap. I love my fiancé and would never cheat on him. Hell, I practice family law, specializing in divorces. I see the damage that cheating leaves behind. There was absolutely no way on God's green earth that I was going to be breaking bread with Gavin. Not now, not ever, right?

"Humility is not thinking of yourself more it's thinking of yourself less."
—Ken Blanchard

Chapter 4

Malcolm

I hated that Troi left for New York the way that she did. I love Troi with all of my heart and soul, but she can work my nerves like nobody's business. To be honest, I'm glad she's gone. I really need a break from all of the bitching, moaning and groaning. We have been getting along so nicely lately and then she had to go and fuck it up. Doesn't she know what kind of pressure I'm under to maintain my record label? I'm trying to put Philly on the map and show the world that Philadelphia has some great hidden talent.

I didn't want to sit in the house and mope all evening, so, although it was Sunday night, I was heading out to an exclusive club for members only in New Jersey. As I checked out my appearance in the full-length mirror, I wondered what drove me to stray from my relationship with Troi, every now and again. Now, don't get me wrong, I'm nobody's dog and there's nothing typical about me, but I can't seem to help myself. The only problem is, now thanks to the damn media, the spotlight is on every brotha in America. I guess I can also

BEWARE OF DOG!

thank that damn E. Lynn Harris and this new author, J.L. King,, these dudes are blowing up my whole game plan with his book On The Down Low and all of the other male-bashing books he's written. I can't help it if I love women, but like the flavor of a strong, thug-type black man every now and again. I know, I know, you can close your damn mouth already. Yes, I'm gon' put it out there. To answer your damn question, yes, I consider myself straight, and no, I don't consider myself gay or bisexual. And you can save the preaching because I know the statistics too. I read the damn newspaper and watch the news. Yes, while it's sad that one in 160 black women are infected with HIV, while only one in 3,000 white women are infected with the virus, it ain't my fault. What about the drug users? I don't see everybody talking about them. It's a pretty upsetting epidemic, but I'm at least doing my part by using condoms. I know that to some folks I must be an asshole and you're probably already wishing that I get mine in the end, but I'm just here to tell you that this shit is not a joke, it's real. Hell, I may be getting ready to go out and screw the hell out of your man. Oh no? Think again. Can you be one hundred percent sure that your man isn't out right now pounding the shit, literally, out of some dude name Jamal? Didn't think so.

You know the first time I was with a guy, was actually in high school. I had a best friend by the name of David Hall, and while I've always been the bookworm type, I was never really a nerd, but was never really the type that would be a football star either. Anyway, David and I grew up in the same Atlanta suburb in Cobb County. One would probably argue that Atlanta is where my love for men all began—who knows, maybe it didn't, but I can't call it. So, David and I would always hang out and then one night, we were over his house eating pizza and drinking beer. We were watching the Atlanta Hawks kick the

BEWARE
OF
DOG!

Cleveland Cavaliers' butts. When halftime came on, David asked if I wanted to watch a porno movie. I hadn't really thought about a movie like that, but David just jumped up and popped the movie in the VCR.

"I'll go get us some more beer. You want one?" I asked.

"Naw man, I'm good," he responded.

"You sure? I know you put some in the freezer awhile ago and they should be icy cold by now." I stated.

"Alright man, I'll take another one," he stated.

David's parents weren't home—in fact, it seemed they were never there and David's two older sisters were married with children, so he was always home alone. So, after a few minutes, I returned downstairs to the den with the beer and was shocked when I entered the room and David was lying in the middle of the den, naked, jerking off.

"Yo, man. What the hell are you doing?" I stated, since David was gasping for breath, apparently about to reach a climax.

"What the fuck does it look like man? I'm jerking my shit off. Either get naked or go the hell back upstairs."

I don't know why I did it, but I unbuttoned my jeans, because I was instantly erect. David just kept on looking at me with a piercing stare and then I began jerking off too. I had been with three girls by then—I was a mere seventeen years old, but I was never into masturbation. My hand and dick never really seemed to get along. The next thing I knew, David jumped up.

"Let me do that for you, man, you're doing it all wrong."

Before I had a chance to protest, David dropped to his knees and took my penis in his mouth and began giving me a blow job. Now, that was a first-time experience for me. None

41

BEWARE
OF
DOG!

of the three girls I had ever had sex with had ever done anything like that to me. I wanted to knock David on his ass and tell him to stop, but the feeling was just so damn good. I couldn't hold it any longer and then finally, I exploded in David's mouth. He turned over and then guided me inside of him and that was a whole different type of experience I'd rather not reveal, but it was eerie because I actually enjoyed it. But, I will say that from that point on, I was kind of hooked. I say kind of because it's not like I'm even attracted to men. I find them repulsive, like the average man would, but I guess I'm attracted to the way a man makes me feel. Plus, sex with a man is probably some of the best sex out there. Men, especially freaks, know how to get down and nasty. I've heard some guys in the life say that only a man knows how to really please a man because a man knows a man's body, and I guess that answers my question on how I got turned out. That doesn't even make sense to me. I like to be turned out by a man every now and then too. But, I'm not gay!

The only problem is that I'm getting married in exactly six months and I still love women. My goal is to get all of this nonsense out of my system before I walk down the aisle. I love Troi, and she's the best thing that ever happened to me. If I ever lost her, I'd probably lose it, mentally that is. Besides, it's not like we're married and we haven't taken any vows yet, so in all actuality, I'm not doing anything wrong. Like I said before, I'm really not attracted to men, so, in my mind that makes me straight, not gay, not bisexual, but like I said earlier, I just like a little flavor every now and again. There's nothing wrong with that, right?

BEWARE OF DOG!

"Early is on time and on time is late."
—Author Unknown

Chapter 5

Corie

Monday morning, while waiting at the traffic light at Twenty-second and Walnut Streets, who do I see sitting at the red light but Malcolm? I beeped my horn, but he didn't see me. I called him on his cell phone because I needed to talk to him about Troi and how he let her leave all upset and what-not. Not that it's any of my business, but I gotta look out for my sista's back. Besides, Malcolm and I needed to sit down and talk numbers.

"Yes!" Malcolm answered his cell phone rather rudely.

"Well good fucking morning to you too."

"Oh, what's up, Corie? I didn't see the name on the Caller I.D."

"Hey, we need to talk," I stated.

"I'm listening," he responded.

"First things first. I need for us to meet up sometime this week. I wanna go over my figures because now is a good time to take The Blue Nile to the next phase," I said.

"When and where do you wanna meet?"

"You tell me. You're the one with the busy schedule."

BEWARE OF DOG!

"How about Wednesday at noon? I can stop at the club, if that's where you're going to be," he responded.

"Sounds like a plan."

"What else is up?" Malcolm asked, still a little too dry for my apples.

"Your future wife. Have you spoken to her since she left yesterday?" I asked.

"She called to let me know she arrived safely, but I didn't really talk to her. Why do you ask?" Malcolm asked, sounding as if he were on the defense.

"'Cause she was pretty upset when she left. Do you mind me asking?"

"It's never stopped you before," Malcolm responded, sounding annoyed.

"Well, since you asked. I think it's fucked up how you let your fiancé get on a damn train to another state, nonetheless and you not even try to make sure that she's alright," I stated.

"I didn't ask and if you hadn't noticed, Troi and I are the engaged couple. People in serious relationships go through this kind of shit from time to time. Don't worry about it. We'll be fine," Malcolm added.

"Well said. From here on out I'm officially out of it. I just wanted to have my say."

"Like I said, it's never stopped you before. Look, I've gotta run. I'll catch you on Wednesday at noon."

"Peace out."

Since investing in The Blue Nile, and advising me on financial matters, Malcolm, Troi and I all agreed that Troi would stay completely out of the business end of things, in an effort to preserve our relationship. If things were to ever go south between Malcolm and me, at least I'd still have my best friend in my corner. Malcolm and I never talk about business with

BEWARE OF DOG!

Troi, and we all like it that way. The only way Troi can become involved is to invest with the rest.

I feel kind of responsible for Malcolm and Troi hooking up. Troi was visiting me at Fisk University, where they first met. I knew the first time I spoke with Malcolm I wanted him to be my business partner because of his ruthlessness. Malcolm is probably the smartest man that I've ever encountered, and I wanted him to become a part of my game plan. He kind of reminded me of a P. Diddy and Suge Knight, wrapped in one. Of course he initially tried to push up on me but I wasn't having that. Never mix business with pleasure. He probably thought that I was interested since I was always up in his face. I definitely wasn't interested; I just wanted to learn as much as I possibly could from him. I asked Malcolm to tutor me, and he still persisted. I would never in a million years date a guy like Malcolm. Don't get me wrong, there's nothing unattractive about him, it's just that I only date men that allow me to be in control, to a certain extent and Malcolm isn't that type of guy. He's the type who when he speaks, he expects you to listen. And I ain't the one. But, when Malcolm met Troi, she had him eating out of the palm of her hand. He once told me that Troi ran the house, but he ran the household. I guess it works for them.

A lot of people have always thought that Troi and I were fraternal twins. We have always been the skinniest girls in the class, you know, small tits and no ass. But, we each grew up and I'm just gon' put it out there, nowadays, we look good. I've been wearing my hair short for the last five years, but I recently started letting it grow out. I now work out faithfully. I even got me a personal trainer. I now am proud to say that I wear a 34D cup, I've got a nice little booty, and I even have a little hip action going. I convinced Troi to work out, too, and now she

BEWARE OF DOG!

has a nice little shape.

After I spoke to Malcolm, I headed over to my club. I had some number figuring to do. I trust Malcolm with my accounts and what have you, but I usually figure things out for myself. I don't let anybody tell me what I can and can't afford and not figure things out for myself, and I always sign my own checks. I don't play when it comes to my money.

Once I completed my figures, King of Prussia Mall was calling me. I jumped in my Range Rover and within twenty minutes I was chilling at my favorite place on Earth, Neiman Marcus. I beat that mall down with a vengeance. I knew that I probably overspent my weekly allowance on my platinum card, but hey, you can't take it with you. As I tried to decide if I was ready to hit a few other stores or head to the gym, my cell phone rang.

"Holla."

"Yo, let's get together for lunch this afternoon." It was my baby Lance Beck.

"When and where?" I asked.

"Normal time and normal place."

"Holla," I said as I confirmed our date for 2:30 PM and ended my call.

I looked at my watch, and it was only one o'clock. I realized that if I pushed it, I still had time to run to the gym and get a quick workout in before my lunch date with Lance. As I was driving my cell phone rang again.

"Holla."

"Why haven't I heard from you?" It was pain-in-the-ass Rashan.

"I just saw you yesterday. What's up?"

"I need to talk to you."

"So talk."

BEWARE OF DOG!

"I wanna see you later on. I'm going through a little something right now with these boys from Delaware and the horn ain't where I wanna holla at you."

"Well it's gon' have to do. I have a busy schedule today and now is about as good as it gets," I replied.

"What you meetin' some nucca? Don't get homie fucked up."

"Look, Shan, I don't have time for your bullshit. What's up?"

"Damn, I ain't worth an hour of your fucking time?"

"I said I'm busy today. Speak now or forever hold your peace," I replied in an annoyed tone.

"You a fucking bitch. I ain't gon' forget about this shit," he said, banging the phone in my ear.

After Rashan ended the call on me, I continued to drive to The Bellevue Fitness Club on Broad and Walnut, arriving there in fifteen minutes flat. I changed into my workout gear, put on my CD Walkman, went around the track for thirty minutes and then got on the stair climber for fifteen minutes before practically collapsing. I really needed to stop working out so hard, but I loved the high I got after a grueling workout. I was so sweaty and nasty. I really needed a massage, but looking at the clock, I realized I had just enough time to shower and head to my spot to meet my baby.

Lance is such a sweetie, but of course I'll never tell him that. I always show him how much I care for him. I love the fact that he can be thugged out when he wants and can be a true gentleman at other times. Our relationship goes way beyond a casual thing. Lance has been married to Sherrie for nine years. Now talk about a weird relationship, but there's no way in the world that I'll ever understand their situation. Lance and I have been together for as much as four days straight. We've taken

BEWARE
OF
DOG!

trips to New York and Atlantic City, and we even flew down to
New Orleans one weekend. Now, I don't know what he told his
wife, but whenever I call, be it at 2:00 AM or 2:00 PM Lance
will come over at the drop of a dime. I try not to be all up in
folks' business, but one time I asked Lance about his situation at
home and he told me what was up. Apparently, Lance's family
has a little bit of change. He comes from a long line of medical
doctors. His grandfather and father were doctors and even his
bourgeois wife is a doctor at University of Pennsylvania, along
with his dad. You see, Lance's people are members of those
bourgeoisie organizations and from where they come, I guess
marriage is more for convenience. Don't get me wrong, my
mother is a member of elite organizations such as the Links and
I was even in Jack and Jill from the time I turned five until I
graduated from high school, but I guess I missed the classes that
say you have to be stuck on stupid, because there's not that
much appearance in the world that would make me put up with
that crap. I'm not one of those "other women" who believes
whatever the man tells me, but trust me, from firsthand
experience, I know what I'm talking about. You see, Sherrie
knows all about me and I know all about her. Girlfriend, I'll
give it to her is smart as hell. I told myself that if I ever wrote a
book, I was going to use this story to educate all of the "other
women."

I had a message at my office one afternoon when I got to
work.

"Hi, it's me. Give me a call when you get this message.
Call me at 555-3434," a woman's voice stated on my voicemail.
I wasn't sure if it was Troi or one of my employees, but I just
couldn't put the voice together. I called the number back and I
said, "Hi, this is Corie. Some one left a message on my
voicemail."

BEWARE OF DOG!

"Hi, Corie. This is Sherrie. Do you know Lance?" she asked casually.

"Uh, yeah," Shit! She busted my ass.

"How well do you know Lance and in what capacity?"

"I guess if you're doing your Sherlock thing then you already know the answer to that."

"I see. How long has this been going on?" she asked.

"Listen, I think you need to take this up with your husband," I stated.

"I have already. He told me that you make him happy."

"Really now?" I questioned suspiciously.

"All I ask is that you two give me some respect. Please don't ever come to my home and please be mindful that my family is very influential in this town and is very well respected. Common courtesy is all that I ask. It's no secret that Lance and I are married to each other in name only. One other thing, I don't expect my husband to bring me back any diseases either. I expect that you're someone very dear to him since he's made that pretty obvious in that he rarely seeks me out for sexual gratitude."

"That's WTMI."

"What's WTMI?" she asked.

"Way too much information," I stated. Damn, she hadn't heard that before?

"Well, as long as you and I know our roles, again, I see nothing wrong with what's going on," she stated.

"Can I ask you a question?" I asked.

"I prefer that we just keep it simple. I'm sure you're wondering why I'm saying all of these things to you, but my business is just that. You and Lance have developed a relationship, and I'd prefer if things were just left the way they are. I'm sure you can respect my privacy," she stated.

49

BEWARE OF DOG!

"Most definitely," I said, at a loss for words.

We hung up and I haven't had a problem with her since. I'm sure that Sherrie discussed things with Lance, but he and I never discussed what had taken place. It was a weird situation but I was satisfied for the moment and Lance and I had a great relationship. I couldn't ask for much more. Was I selling myself short? No, my needs were being met and due to my past issues, it was all that I wanted.

My thoughts of Lance were interrupted when my cell phone rang. My phone was lodged down in my pocketbook so as I was retrieving it I hit the answer button without getting a look at the Caller I.D.

"Holla."

"Why didn't you call me back?" It was Rashan.

"I don't believe you had the audacity to call me back," I said.

"I need to rap with you. I'm under a lot of stress right now."

"So that gives you the right to call me a bunch of names?" I asked, irritated.

"Listen, I need to put my hands on some extra cheddar."

"And what does that have to do with me? Get to the point."

"I can't holla on the horn. Where you gon' be in an hour? I'ma come through your spot."

"I know you aren't asking me for money."

"Damn, why don't you just blast me all over the damn horn. You gon' get up wit' me or not?" Rashan stated, equally irritated.

"Not."

"Oh, so I ain't worth an hour of your precious time?"

"Look, Rashan, I don't have time for the small talk. I

BEWARE OF DOG!

said, speak now or forever hold your peace."

"There you go getting outta pocket again. Learn to shut your fucking pie hole for a minute. Damn, you act like a fucking man all of the time."

"You know that I'm just a gay man in a woman's body. That's been my M.O. since day one. Ain't nothing changed."

"Well then, I'm gon' bust your ass in the mouth since you're so much of a fucking man. See how you like that," the asshole stated, banging the phone in my ear. Screw him.

I arrived at Ms. Tootsie's and Lance was already there, looking good as ever. I really do love Lance because he's so good to me. Besides, he has his own money and I have mine, which makes him so much more attractive. I don't feel superior or inferior to him. It's probably a good thing he is married, because a couple like us would never make it living all happily married ever after and shit since we both like to be in control. Naw, I like it just the way it is.

"Hey baby," I said as I walked up and gave Lance a kiss on the forehead. As long as Lance and I have been together, we've never kissed on the lips. I don't believe in kissing on the lips. Way too personal.

"What's up?"

"You order for me?"

"You know I did."

I waved to my buddy, Andre', who's the manager and who hold's it down for the owner, KeVen Parker. He's muscular, dark chocolate and sometimes wears his hair in some sexy-ass dreads. To put it mildly, he's fine as hell, but he ain't got nothing on my baby Lance. Andre came over and kissed me on the cheek. We chitchatted for a few minutes and then our food came so I had to cut the conversation short. I was so hungry after that workout that I could have eaten a damn cow.

BEWARE OF DOG!

No, make that two cows. Lance ordered me the grilled salmon salad and a large iced tea, my favorite meal at Ms. Tootsie's. Whoever arrives at the restaurant first orders the meal. That's the beauty of us, we know each other so well.

After we ate and talked for a while, Lance asked, "What do you have planned for the rest of the day?"

"You're coming back to my place to give me the massage that I missed by meeting you here for lunch."

"We're out. Let's bounce."

Lance followed me back to my house and as I pulled up in my driveway, something told me to turn to the left. Who do I see parked on the corner of the next block? You guessed it, Rashan. I played it real cool though. Lance pulled into the second garage since my car was still in the shop. Mental note, call those bastards and see when my car is being released. Anyway, my cell phone rang instantly, so I turned it off. I never gave Rashan my home telephone number and now thinking about it, giving him my home address was obviously a big mistake. I had to make sure that if I didn't handle anything else, I had to cut Rashan off and real soon. He was beginning to get on my last nerve. But for now, I wasn't going to let anything come between me and my massage from Lance. The man should be a masseuse because he has all the right moves, and my bones were aching.

Lance serviced me just right all afternoon and then we both fell asleep. I woke up around six and realized that I had to get to the club. Mondays are pretty busy for me since its poetry night. Don't let me ever try to cancel on the Philly poets; I just may have a real riot on my hands. They live to get on that damn microphone.

Lance bounced with me and I headed over to the club. My manager, Vanita Kennedy, had opened up the spot and was

setting up. She had the night shift coming in a half hour and had one of the guys helping her out with unloading all of the boxes and what-not. From the looks of things, Vanita was really working out and I had realized that I made the right choice in promoting her to manager. I believe in keeping my employees happy.

By 9:00 PM the regulars started cramming in, and an hour later the place was jam packed. Yes, it was definitely time to take The Blue Nile to the next level. That's why I desperately needed to speak with Malcolm so we could go over the figures. My investors were pleased with the increased profits, and I had a few more lined up that wanted to get in on the action.

At 11:30 the poetry readings ended and the place started thinning out. I retrieved the cash from the front door and the four cash registers around the four bars and went upstairs to my office..I locked the door when I was safely inside and placed the money in my hidden safe box. Not even Malcolm knew where I kept my funds. The only living soul that I'd ever told was Troi—oh yeah, and my parents. As soon as I reentered the room, someone knocked on the door with the secret code that I had in place. I had to take these precautions because there are too many haters out there waiting for me to slip off my game.

I went back behind my desk. "Who is it?" I asked.

"It's Rashan."

Now was as good a time as any to cut this motherfucker from my life. Since I had to do it anyway, I'd rather it was at the club, you know witnesses and everything. I made sure that my 10mm was securely on my waistband and the safety lock was off. That's right, the heat is on at all times. Fuck that, 22 bullshit. That's for girly girls and I ain't one of them by a long shot.

BEWARE OF DOG!

After I purchased my gun, I began going to the range so much, the police officers tried to recruit me for the police department as a sniper. Trust me I can hold my own.

I buzzed Rashan in, and when he walked in I knew there was going to be trouble. I don't know if I mentioned this, but Rashan is a few cans shy of a six pack. He ain't wrapped too tight. But when they made his crazy ass they made an even crazier one, me. Rashan better not start his nonsense, because I was going to finish it.

"I see you had a nice little afternoon with that motherfucker. I thought I told you to stay away from him," he stated with an evil snarl on his thugged-out face.

"Who the fuck do you think you're talking to, Rashan?" I asked.

"You better watch your damn mouth. I done told you about that mouth."

"Let me tell you one," before I could finish my sentence the bastard smacked the shit out of me. I ain't gon' lie, that smack stung my lip, and it was instantly swollen. I touched my lip and noticed blood in the corner of my mouth. It took me a second to regain my senses. I think I was in shock. Suddenly, Rashan jumped over my desk and began choking me.

"You wanna be a fucking hard-ass? This is what I do to motherfuckers…" He never got a chance to finish his sentence.

I slowly pulled my glock from my waistband and held it to Rashan's chin. There's no other feeling in this world like a cold piece of steel that tells a person that you mean business. I promise you that cold steel is a universal feeling. Rashan released his chokehold on me, like I knew that he would, because he knows that I would have shot his ass dead where he stood.

"I'm going to say this one time and one time only. Get

BEWARE OF DOG!

the fuck out of my club, and I don't ever want to see your fucking face again. You hit me once, bitch, but you'll never have that experience again. Chalk that one up to a freebie. You hear me?"

"Loud and clear," Rashan said, looking me directly in the eye as he backed out the door.

I know the guys I mess around with and I knew Rashan's next move would be to probably try to put the fear of God in me. I knew that I had merely caught him off guard, but the next time I wouldn't catch him slipping. I didn't know how it was coming, but I knew that now more than ever I had to stay up on my P's and Q's, right?

"Stop trying to see what your eyes can't follow."
—Keith Murray, Rapper

Chapter 6

Troi

Monday morning came too soon. I slept so good, and that was really a surprise to me, because normally when I sleep in a hotel, I find it hard to get comfortable with my surroundings. I had the best dream about Gavin. It was so bad and I felt so guilty about it.

I dreamed that I met him in the elevator, and of course the elevator got stuck on the thirteenth, of all floors. We looked at each other and he began smiling. I smiled back and the next thing I know I walked up to him and began unbuttoning his shirt. I kissed on his chest, which was full of little curls. Not the hard, tight curls, but soft, loose ones that were calling my lips to them. Gavin pressed his hard, muscle-toned body up against mine and then took his left hand and pulled up my dress. He began rubbing all over my ass and then he dropped to his knees. He slid my thong down to my ankles, and I stepped out of it. He placed it under his nose and moaned loudly. He put my thong in his pocket and then gently placed his mouth over the lips of my vagina.

I began quivering and shivering as I thought, This man's

mouth should be patented. Just when I didn't think I could stand it anymore, he abruptly stopped and took off his suit jacket and laid it down on the floor. He helped me on his suit jacket and continued his morning snack. I felt as if I was about to pass out. Gavin took his strong, hard hands and opened each side of my vagina and took his tongue and licked slowly yet gently on each side. So delicately that I wonder where he learned how to be so gentle to a woman. Again, was I passing out?

He then inserted his middle finger deeply inside of me. He removed his finger and began licking it, while he continued to moan out loud. If I didn't know any better I'd say he was at a party all by himself. He began his feast again. By this time I had juices running down my leg because he was truly enjoying and devouring me. He abruptly stopped tasting me and he kneeled, unbuttoning his pants, removing his penis. It's the blackest penis I've ever seen and the most beautiful. I thought, there was no way that thing is going to fit in me, but I was up for the challenge. He began to straddle me, but then I wanted to taste him as well. While he was still kneeling, I moved down even farther and placed my mouth over his shaft. I tried the deep-throat technique, but I'm no porn star. I damn near choked. I tried my best to give him the same pleasure that he gave me. I inserted my middle finger in his rectum and he started to lose control. I began to feel that little vein pop up down at the base of his penis, and I know he's about to climax, so I stop, 'cause I don't swallow. That's nasty! I shimmy back up and I place each leg well past each ear, I want him to feel all of me. Just as he's about to enter me, the alarm goes off! I hate when that happens. I tried like hell to go back to sleep because I wanted to know what happened. Unfortunately, it was over. Damn! Damn! Damn!

BEWARE OF DOG!

I dragged myself out of bed and brewed some coffee. If I don't have my coffee I ain't good to nobody. Talk about bitch on wheels. Anyway, I called Jennifer, and we agreed to meet in the hotel lobby around eight so we could catch a taxi together uptown for our seminar.

I got dressed, putting on my cute little red silk dress with the matching jacket. I applied my lipstick and was ready to meet the world. I have never worn anything other than lipstick. I have the most evenly toned skin, that to wear foundation would be a sin. Most women, especially my girlfriends who must wear makeup, hate hard on this fact, but don't hate the playa…you know the rest.

As I walked down the hallway, who comes out of his door, looking and smelling all too good, but Gavin? Ummh. And that suit had to be tailor made. I looked at him from head to toe, and let me just put it out there, I wanted to rip every stitch of clothing off him and make my earlier dream come true. Alright, I'm better now. Anyway, he started smiling like he had in my dream. Like he had a front row seat in my head. I got wet right then and there.

"Good morning," I said casually, trying like hell to be cool with mine.

"It is now."

"That's the best you can come up with?" I said, walking past him.

"Damn. Do you always look this good?" he asked.

"You should see me when I wake up." I wish that I could have retracted that comment.

"I'm trying to."

"I walked right into that one, huh?"

"So, will tonight be the night?" he asked as he stood closely behind me as I pressed the elevator button and waited. I

BEWARE OF DOG!

could feel his strong chest up against my back.

"The night for what?" I asked, trying to play like I didn't know what he was talking about.

"The night that I get to take you out to dinner?"

Before I could answer, the elevator arrived, and there were four people on. I got in and scooted to the side. Gavin squeezed directly behind me, and this time I felt his entire body pressed against mine. I felt his penis against my back, and I was appalled and excited at the same time. I couldn't move an inch. He had me trapped and didn't utter one word. I tried to cut my eye at him, without anyone noticing, but he simply looked up and began whistling.

Everyone filed off the elevator and Gavin got off with them, still whistling that damn tune. I guess he figured two could play the little cat-and-mouse game. And guess what? It was working. He had thrown a hook on a sista.

When I got off the elevator, I saw Jennifer by the door, and she waved and yelled for me to hurry along. I walked briskly to the front of the lobby, exited the doors and got in the cab she had waiting. I felt that Gavin was looking, but I refused to look back.

Throughout the day, the seminar was truly challenging. Way too much information was being thrown to us at one time, but it was cool because I got to see so many of my colleagues whom I hadn't seen in such a long while, so all of the various exercises were worth it. To make matters even better, our facilitator let us out early so Diana, my girl from New York; Jennifer and I hit downtown Manhattan for the department store sales.

I absolutely love to shop, and Corie is about the only person who enjoys it just as much as me. I bought so many clothes that I really contemplated cutting up my platinum card

BEWARE OF DOG!

into millions of little pieces, but I only get to New York about three times a year so I had to make the most of it. We all grabbed a slice of pizza and then agreed that we were all shopped out. Jennifer and I caught a cab back to the hotel, but not before promising Dee that we'd have dinner at her house and that we'd be there by 7:30. I truly wasn't feeling that whole woman bonding thang because I just wanted to paint the town all night long.

When I got back to my hotel room, I noticed that I didn't have any messages. I was really disappointed that Malcolm hadn't called, but I damn sure wasn't calling his stubborn ass. I took a quick shower, changed into a denim mini dress and my denim sandals and was ready to do the exhale thang with the girls—well, not really, but this was as good as it was going to get.

Down in the lobby, I waited for Jennifer and who comes strolling in? You guessed it, Gavin.

"You were waiting for me, huh?" he asked.

"How'd you guess? It was suppose to be a surprise," I teased.

"So, I guess no dinner for us tonight," he stated.

Thankfully, Jennifer walked up and grabbed me by the arm.

"Hey, girl. You ready? Hi, I'm Jennifer. How are you?"

"I'm just some lonely guy that Troi won't have dinner with tonight."

"Well she's crazy," Jennifer teased.

"You ready?" I asked, growing impatient.

"You two have a good night," Gavin said, walking away, trying not to look sad.

As we waited outside of the hotel for a taxi, Jennifer

60

BEWARE OF DOG!

tried to jump all up in my business.

"Girl, why don't you have dinner with him? I can tell Dee you made other plans."

"Because I don't even know him and besides he's too dangerous. You see how fine he is?" I asked as the cab pulled up to the curb.

"That's why you should be going. You only live once. Enjoy yourself."

"That kind of enjoyment can land me in divorce court before I even walk down the aisle. That's alright, I'm chillin' on safe mode with my girls," I responded.

We took the twenty-five-minute drive to Brooklyn and by the time we arrived at Dee's apartment, I was starving. Diana had prepared Spanish peas and rice, grilled chicken and lots and lots of white wine. By the time we had finished eating and reminiscing, the wine had taken its effect on me, and I really wanted to hit the clubs of New York, not sit up in some damn apartment.

"Dee, you know any clubs that are jumping on Monday nights?" I asked.

"Not really. There are a few, but I'm not sure what type of crowds are there are on Mondays."

"The bellman told me about this one club on Forty-sixth and Eight. Club Word. I think that's the name he said. He told me Monday nights were jumping with a mixed crowd. You guys wanna go?" Jennifer asked.

"I'm down. If I sit here any longer, I'm going to be drooling on your sofa. I gotta get moving," I said, ready to go.

"Well I figured we could just have a few drinks and just chill for tonight," Dee said.

"No harm, Diana, but we came to get our party on," Jennifer stated in her southern drawl.

BEWARE OF DOG!

"Well you two can go, but I'm going to stay here. I'm not feeling that club scene tonight. We can all go out before you guys leave. Thursday is mambo night at a club uptown that I go to. You guys go on and have a good time. I'm chillin'," Dee stated.

"You sure?" I asked.

"Yeah, I'm pretty tired. Y'all be safe out there. I'll catch up to you later on tomorrow," Dee said.

Jennifer and I said our good-byes and just like that we were pardoned from dinner. We were sitting at Club Word thirty minutes later, waving the bartender down for apple martinis. It was a pretty live crowd, and the music was blaring the new Janet Jackson song. I wanted to get my drink and then tear up the dance floor. As I flagged the bartender, Jennifer pulled some Asian guy to the floor, and they started ripping it up. Suddenly, I felt these large hands over my eyes. I hoped it wasn't Jennifer because that meant she had some rough-ass hands.

"Guess who?" The hands fell. I turned around and it was Gavin.

"That's it. I'm calling the police. You're stalking me," I teased.

"Never that. What are you doing here? Too good to go to dinner with me and now you're trying to get picked up in a club?" Gavin teased.

"Never that. We just got here. We had dinner plans with one of our girls and decided we wanted to get our groove on. No harm in that, is it?" I asked.

"Why are you sitting here? Let's go," Gavin said, pulling me to the dance floor. We must have danced for an hour straight, and that confirmed my thoughts. I was in love. Well, maybe not love, but definitely lust. There's nothing better than

BEWARE OF DOG!

a good-looking, good-dressing and good-smelling man, except for a good-dancing man. We kicked it and I knew that heaven had sent him straight from the clouds. We were made for each other—well the wife and fiancé thing kept getting in the way.

We found Jennifer and she was all hugged up with this fine-ass white dude, whom I later found out was named Paul, from Birmingham, Alabama. I wasn't mad at her. Come to find out he was with Gavin and a few of them had come together. Apparently, the same bellman that informed Jennifer about Club Word had informed Gavin and his crew.

Gavin and I pulled up to the table where Jennifer and Paul were cuddled up and within a few minutes, Paul had us dying with laughter at his stupid jokes. I was enjoying myself and never even thought about the time.

"I'm hungry. What do you all say we blow this joint and grab something to eat before we call it a night?" Jennifer suggested.

"That's what's up. I'm starving," I added.

We bounced to this all-night diner. I ordered the home fries and cheese omelet. Our food came within minutes and to say that I literally inhaled it was an understatement. I was starving and wasn't embarrassed to show it.

"Just what I love, a woman who loves to eat," Gavin leaned over and whispered in my ear before shoving a forkful of pancakes in his mouth.

"Um-hmm," I muttered through a stuffed mouth.

After we ate, Gavin picked up the bill and we bounced back over to the hotel. We must have looked like four drunks walking in the lobby. There was no one there, except for hotel security. We each showed our room key and he just nodded and went back to reading his paper.

We all piled onto the elevator and when we reached

BEWARE OF DOG!

Paul's floor, Jennifer gave him a good-night kiss that I'm sure her husband wouldn't have appreciated. When we arrived at Jennifer's floor, Gavin and I held the elevator to make sure she arrived at her room safely.

Gavin and my floor arrived, and as we stepped off the elevator, he grabbed my hand and continued walking past his door. I was surely hoping this guy wasn't going to play himself.

"Don't worry, I'm just escorting you to your room to make sure you get in safely. I'm not going to try anything. You can stop worrying now," Gavin stated. He was definitely reading my mind.

We arrived at my room and I placed my key card in the door. I could feel Gavin up against my back and I could also feel that his penis was growing with excitement, but then so was I.

"Gavin, I had a great time tonight. You're a lot of fun to hang out with."

"But not quite good enough for you to have dinner with me, right?" he asked.

"I never said that."

"What about a good-night kiss then?" he asked.

"Uh, news flash, you're married and I have a fiancé," I stated, knowing full well that I wanted him to grab me by the back of the neck and kiss me like Malcolm used to before he became an asshole. Now, don't get me wrong, I think cheating is dead wrong. It ain't nothing right about it. I'm a respectable and prominent attorney, and I love my fiancé. I've never even had any thoughts about creepin' with someone else. If all this were true, then why did I want Gavin so badly?

He must have read my mind because next thing I know, he was moving in closely. The door was partially open, and he pressed up against me and began kissing me gently at first and

64

BEWARE
OF
DOG!

then hard and passionate, just what I wanted and needed at that very moment. I pulled him toward me and began moving backward, dragging him in my hotel suite. I backed us both against the living room wall, and he cupped my face in his huge hands. We continued kissing feverishly, pulling each other's clothes off, as if we hadn't a care in the world. I don't know how it happened next but we were both stripped down to our underwear, and I was pushing him on the king-size bed, straddling him. I began gyrating my hips and then he began trying to remove my thong. This was near impossible since I was on top of him. I grabbed each of his wrists and held them firmly on the bed. I was in control. I began removing his T-shirt and sucking on his nipples. Just then, the phone rang.

"Oh shit," I said as I jumped up from the bed.

"Hold on. Get yourself together first."

"Good idea," I replied. My heart was beating a mile per minute. The phone rang three more times before I answered.

"Yeah," I answered in a fake sleepy voice.

"Stop faking it. I've known you long enough," Corie yelled into the phone.

"Girl, what the hell do you want? Do you know what time it is?" I asked, beginning to regain my composure.

I gave Gavin the thumbs-up to let him know it wasn't Malcolm and I could see a look of relief on his face.

"I'm downstairs. Why didn't you tell the front desk that I was coming?" Corie asked.

"I didn't know you were coming. You said you might come up this week. Why didn't you call to let me know what was up?" I asked, becoming confused.

"I see you didn't check your voicemail. Girl, just talk to the damn manager and tell him it's okay to let me up. We can chitchat later," Corie said, putting the night manager on the

BEWARE OF DOG!

phone.

Gavin, obviously listening to my conversation, began getting dressed. I hung up with the manager and knew that he had to hurry up before Corie arrived.

"I guess the party's over," I said.

"Yeah, I'd better go. I hope you'll still consider going out to dinner with me."

"I'll call you tomorrow," I lied.

"Stay sweet," he said, kissing me on the forehead before he headed down the hallway to his room.

Within three minutes, Corie was knocking on the door. I opened it and she came bursting through, typical Corie style.

"Nice to see you, too, trick," I stated.

"Your mama. This is a really nice suite," Corie replied, putting her bags down by the sofa.

We gave each other a hug and that's where I goofed.

"Aw shit. I smell men's cologne. Is that Oxygen? Do tell."

"Tell what?" I tried to conceal my deceit.

I normally tell Corie just about everything, but this was different. You see, I've always been on Corie about dating married men, telling her how wrong it was and here I was. Look at me. Acting a fool up in here.

"You know, you're not a good liar. First of all, you're still in your clothes at three in the damn morning, and I know a man's cologne when I smell it. Now are you going to tell me what's going on or do I have to beat the shit out of you?"

"Wait a damn minute. What are you doing rolling up here at 3:00 AM anyway? What brings you here so late?" I asked.

"Long story," Corie replied. Her demeanor changed.

"Alright. I'll tell you my secret if you tell me yours

first," I responded.

Needless to say, when two best friends get together and begin talking about men, the outcome is going to always be a long one. Let's just say I didn't get to bed until 4:30. I was surprised when I told Corie about Gavin. She didn't judge me, but it was the unsaid that was so important. She was pretty much telling me that one should never say what they wouldn't do, because the same thing you said you'd never do is the same thing you find yourself doing.

"So, what are you going to do about this Gavin character?" Corie asked.

"Nothing. I'm not going to see him anymore while I'm here."

"Whatever," Corie responded.

"Yeah, well, what are you going to do about Rashan?" I asked.

"Just lay low. I know he's going to start his shit, but I figured I'd let him cool down first. No sense in adding fuel to the fire. I just have to make sure I keep my hip heavy," Corie stated, referring to her gun.

"Just be careful, girl. I never liked his crazy ass anyway. He's a little too thugged out for even you."

"You know that's the way I like 'em."

"I know if anybody can handle this situation, it's you. I just want you to just be careful, girl. Now, on that note, I'm taking my ass to bed. I have to get up in three hours. Nighty-night," I said, heading to my bedroom.

"But you didn't give me a good-night kiss yet," she teased.

"You're nasty," I said, slamming the door on Corie and getting in my bed. I was happy my sista-friend was chilling in New York with me, away from crazy Rashan.

BEWARE OF DOG!

When the alarm blared at 7:30 AM, I thought that I had died and gone straight to hell. I finally dragged myself out of bed after hitting the snooze button three times. Thankfully, my clothes didn't need to be ironed and all I had to do was shower and pull my hair tightly in a ponytail. I called Jennifer and she sounded just as horrible, and we agreed to meet in the lobby at 8:30.

I peeked in to Corie's room, and she was sound asleep. I wanted to go in there and shake her simple. I was so jealous that she got to sleep the day away, but instead, I closed the door and left a message on the refrigerator to call me on my cell phone if she needed anything.

Jennifer and I met exactly at the predetermined time in the lobby. We hailed our taxi and were whisked away uptown to our seminar.

"I'm so damn tired," Jennifer complained in the taxi.

"Tired is not the word. At least you got about five hours of sleep. Corie came up after I left you and I didn't get to sleep until 4:30 AM," I responded.

"Well you got an hour's more sleep than me."

"But I left you around 2:30," I stated.

"I went up to Paul's room. We didn't do anything. We just kissed and talked all night long."

"Who am I to judge? You're a grown woman," I said, knowing that my night could have been just as sinful, had Corie not shown up.

"Girl, Paul's the bomb. We're supposed to meet up at the sports bar tonight around nine. I had so much fun with you guys last night, but I need to get some sleep first," Jennifer stated.

"I'm coming straight back to the hotel tonight and going straight to sleep, no hanging out for me."

BEWARE OF DOG!

"Yeah right," Jennifer teased.

"Watch," I stated.

We rode the next few minutes in silence, probably because we both fell asleep. Next thing, the taxi driver was waking us up and telling us to pay up in his Middle Eastern accent.

Our next seminar was grueling. Have you ever had to stay awake and listen to presenter after presenter, especially on a day after you've been hanging out all night long? I promise you, it's no day at the beach, and I wouldn't try it if I were you.

Finally, 4:30 PM rolled around and we were released. I tried to get Jennifer's attention, but she and Diana were talking to some folks and I was definitely in bitch mode and didn't have time to wait around. I had a bed with my name on it. I walked outside and couldn't even enjoy the summer breeze because I was just so damn tired. I thought of taking the train, but I just wanted to get back to my room—quick, fast and in a hurry. Within fifteen minutes I was back at the hotel, in my room and ready to get under the bed to catch some z's.

I checked my voicemail and still didn't have a message from that fiancé of mine. I was beginning to think I didn't even have a man at this point. How could Malcolm not even call me to make sure I was alright? Later for that. I was too tired to think about all that drama.

Corie had left a message stating that she had hooked up with one of her friends from college and had gone off to do some shopping. Wonderful. No noise from big mouth.

I got in the bed and knocked out. That was probably one of the best naps I'd had in a long time. I awakened around 8:30 PM to the annoying sounds of the telephone blaring in my ear.

"Alright, sleeping beauty. You've had enough sleep. Wake up and get down here. Gavin is looking for you,"

BEWARE OF DOG!

Jennifer yelled into the receiver over the loud music coming from the hotel sports bar.

"Girl, please. There's no way in the world that I'm coming down there. I'm going back to sleep. Now leave me alone," I demanded.

"Sorry, that's not going to happen. You promised me we'd hang out all week."

"Jenn, for real. I'm tired. I can't hang like I used to."

"So what am I supposed to tell Gavin?"

"Tell him to go home to his wife," I said.

"Not funny."

"Peace out," I said, beginning to hang up the phone.

"I'll call you back in an hour," Jennifer said as she hung up the phone in my ear.

If it's one thing that I can't stand, that's to be awakened from a sound sleep and not be able to fall back to sleep. I laid there for another ten minutes, hearing all kinds of sirens, horns honking and just plain old New York noise. Since I live in downtown Philadelphia, this normally doesn't bother me, but it kind of reminded me of home and the thought of still not really talking to Malcolm. I got out of bed and went into the living room and looked down the twenty-three flights onto the busy street. I sat down and contemplated what to do.

Enough was enough, Malcolm should be home, either watching some sort of sports news or working in his den. I would have to be the bigger person and break down and call him. It wouldn't be the first time and it probably wouldn't be the last that I had to be the bigger person to make our relationship more solid.

I carefully dialed the number and the phone rang three times before Malcolm answered.

"Hello, hello," Malcolm said, answering the phone out

BEWARE OF DOG!

of breath.

"Hey, what's up?"

"Uh, nothing. What's up with you?" Malcolm stated, still breathing heavily.

"Why are you so out of breath?" I asked.

"I was halfway out the door, but then I ran back in when I heard the phone ringing."

Just then, Corie came bursting through the door in traditional Corie fashion, and when she noticed I was on the phone she went into the kitchen.

"Oh, where are you headed to this time of night?" I asked calmly.

"I have a meeting with Corie. I saw her earlier today, but I didn't have all of the figures she requested, so I was on my way over there to drop those off."

"Oh, you're meeting Corie tonight?" I asked as Corie was coming out of the kitchen and almost choked on the water she was drinking.

"How is Corie doing? I haven't spoken to her all week. I'll probably just talk to her when I get back," I continued, playing Malcolm right out of the box.

"Alright, I don't want to hold you up. I'll talk to you later on."

"Yeah, let me go, I want to get back here and get some rest. I've got a long day tomorrow."

"Love you," I said, just to see what he would say.

"Yeah, me too. Gotta go. See ya," he said, and just like that he banged the phone in my ear.

I hadn't even hung up the phone, and from the look on Corie's face, she was fuming.

"What the hell is going on? I know your damn man didn't just use me for one of his lies."

71

BEWARE OF DOG!

"Sure did," I stated calmly.

"I can have us back in Philly in an hour and a half. We can roll up on that motherfucker and bust his ass," Corie stated.

"I'm cool," I said, getting up and going into the bathroom.

I could hear Corie rambling. "I can't believe this asshole is starting this shit again."

I came out to the living room and sat down on the sofa adjacent to Corie. "Now don't forget, he didn't actually sleep with that woman. Remember? He just happened to have a receipt for some flowers that weren't sent to me. Remember that?" I stated, referring to some drama Malcolm and I had been through in the past. "And let's not forget that time the other woman kept calling my house until I got that damn Caller I.D. and didn't tell him. Remember that too? Why the fuck did I agree to marry him in the first place? This marriage would be a fucking joke," I said, becoming more enraged by the second. I wanted to kill something, and fast.

"I'm feeling really angry right about now with him lying on me and I can't say a damn thing to him." Corie stated.

"But you know what? Fuck him. I'm done. Mark this day in your Palm Pilot. This is the day that I am mentally through with Malcolm. I'm never going to bring this issue up to him. I'm just out, and you can count on that," I said, getting up and heading to my room. I laid out a pair of white shorts and black midriff tank top. I got in the shower and tried to wash away the anger.

I must have stayed in the shower for what seemed like a million years. As much as I wanted to cry, no tears would formulate. I got out of the shower and pulled out my favorite bay rum shea butter lotion and my Organza perfume. Malcolm had bought the whole Organza gift set for me when we went to

BEWARE OF DOG!

Paris last year. I should have left his ass a long time ago. But you know, women can play the fool one time too many sometimes.

I quickly dressed and exited the room.

"You alright?" Corie asked.

"Yup. Just fine."

"Where are you going?"

"I'm going down to the sports bar. You coming?"

"Naw, if you don't need me, I'm going to stay right here. I see enough of the inside of a bar each and every night. I'm going to read one of these books that I bought from the bookstore and try on all of these damn clothes that I bought and just relax," Corie stated.

"You sure, you're alright?"

"After I go and get Gavin, I'll be just fine," I said.

"Girl, don't fuck no man because your fiancé is screwing you over. Trust me, some women ain't cut out for that shit. You'll be the one hurting in the long run," Corie advised.

"From this day forward, I don't have any feelings. Now, if there's going to be any fucking, it's going to be me doing it. I'm living on my terms now. It's all about me, and trust me when I tell you I can handle it."

"My dawg. Take these," Corie said, going into her purse, pulling out four female condoms. She tossed them to me. I put them in my purse and headed for the door.

"Don't wait up."

"Fuck you. You don't have to rub it in," Corie stated.

"Hate doesn't look good on you," I teased.

"I'm here for you," she said.

"Don't go getting all how you doing? on me," I responded.

"Never that. Now get out. I've got rest to get. Peace,

73

BEWARE
OF
DOG!

and be careful. And do everything that I'd do."

"That could take all night," I replied.

I headed on down to the sports bar and it was jam packed. I found Jennifer, Paul and Gavin with a bunch of other folks in the back at a huge round table. Jennifer was again feeling it, and I wondered if I needed to call A.A. on her. She was just a dancing and singing, but I wasn't mad at her. At least she was having a good time. Eleven years of a terrible marriage and two kids later can bring out the beast in Mrs. Cleaver.

I got Jennifer's attention, ignoring the intensive stare that Gavin was giving me. He obviously thought I was paying him no mind. I pulled Jennifer to the side of the bar. "Hey listen, I'm going to bounce. I have mad drama going on, so I'll check out tomorrow or something, but at least I showed my face," I said.

"I love you, girl. I'm having such a wonderful time. I Love New York!" Jennifer screamed as everyone else held up their drinks and started hooting and hollering, as only white folks can do so well. She was definitely off the hook.

It was pretty obvious that Jennifer was drunk and was in good hands with Paul. I walked over to Gavin and whispered in his ear. "I want you to meet me at your room in five minutes. I want to fuck you." He played it really cool and just nodded, as I had just given him a great piece of information. Little did he know I was about to give him a great piece alright. I walked back over to Jennifer and whispered in her ear. "Alright, snap out of it. I'm leaving. Are you going to be okay?" I asked.

"Yeah, girl. I've only had three beers. You just don't know how good it is to be free. Don't get me wrong, I'm feeling it, but I'm cool. Go, take care of your business. I'm going to sit here and keep drinking these beers these guys are buying. I'm fine," Jennifer promised.

BEWARE OF DOG!

After our brief talk, I felt confident that Jennifer was really not that drunk. So I took the elevator to the twenty-third floor to Gavin's room. I was about to knock on his door and then it hit me: I couldn't sleep with this man. That just wasn't me. I turned to walk away and then the door swung open. I can't say that I wasn't a bit nervous. After all, if he said the right thing, who knows what I would have done? On one hand there was nothing right about sleeping with someone who was married. I mean how can you possibly justify that? I mean, centuries ago, a woman would have been stoned to her death for the act of adultery. But, on the other hand, I just couldn't describe how badly I needed this fling, this one time. After all I wasn't the one who was married. Then again, isn't that why men have so much flexibility to cheat now, because of women like me who don't think twice about the unsuspecting wife? Who does the responsibility belong to anyway? Decisions, decisions.

Gavin stood there with his eyes piercing my skin. I had to admit he utterly surprised me by answering the door in only a towel. His muscular body was glistening from the quick shower he had just taken. Who knew that under that tailor-made suit was a body of a Greek god look-alike. I've seen some pecks in my day, but, damn! I had to regain my composure. I had to remember who was in charge here. I couldn't be drooling all over my tank top for heaven's sake.

"Where are you going? You're not bailing out on me, are you?"

"Yeah, I am. I can't make a mistake like this. This is wrong."

"Come on, baby. Nobody has to ever know. Come inside and let me make you feel good. I bet your pussy tastes like strawberries," he said.

BEWARE OF DOG!

"Naw, I'm going to pass. Although the offer sounds inviting, I'd just be using you," I said.

He looked around to see if anyone was present and then he removed his towel, exposing all of himself to me. "Use me baby. I don't mind," he said.

I was totally speechless because I was so glad to have gotten that warning. This brotha was hung so low that I knew that he would have ripped my insides to shreds. No thanks. I mean, he had to be every bit—and I'm not exaggerating—of ten inches and that was soft.

"Oh, hell no. I'm cool," I said, as I began walking back to my room.

"I know I'm packing, but you sure I can't offer you a night you'll never forget. I can do some awesome things with this tongue of mine," he said.

"I'm sure you can. No thanks," I said, arriving at my room and thanking myself for not making a mistake that I was sure I'd find myself regretting for the rest of my life.

When I arrived at the room, Corie was in bed sleeping and I went inside and thought long and hard about what lay ahead of me with my relationship with Malcolm—or lack thereof. I had no idea what was going on with him but a little voice inside told me things were going to get a whole lot worse before they got better. I had to brace myself for the unknown, whatever it was going to be, but whatever the outcome I had made the right decision with Gavin, right?

"Without communication there is silence."
—Zen Buddha

Chapter 7

Corie

I had been in New York since early Tuesday, and I guess I'm just not the type of person to do that relaxing shit. Besides, I have a damn business to run. With Malcolm playing my girl, his fiancé, ain't no telling what the fuck he was doing. Don't get me wrong, Troi is my best friend, but she can hold her own. My money can't. I was anxious to get back to Philly to see how my funds were doing. I'm not one to trust a whole lot of people, but gut instinct told me Malcolm was up to more than just creeping. I just hoped that he wasn't fucking Troi and me over 'cause best friend or not, I'd have to bust his ass.

Since it was already Thursday, I was supposed to hang out with Troi and her square-ass friends that night, but I decided to head on home and face the unknown, whatever it might be. Corie Simms doesn't run from nobody, man or woman.

I figured I'd wait for Troi to meet her co-worker and then leave her a note for Troi on the fridge, explaining I had an emergency at the club. That wasn't really a lie. My club needed me and I needed it, so that constituted an emergency. I left the hotel around 9:00 AM, checked my Range out of valet

BEWARE OF DOG!

parking and fought my way to the Holland Tunnel. I was going home to face the music.

I was jamming on my way home, I was listening to Wendy Williams' radio show, The Wendy Williams Experience and she was updating me on the latest gossip. After I was all caught up I began listening to my oldies. Many people say that I've got an old soul. Most of my friends, including Troi, listen to that damn rap and reggae crap, but give me my Marvin, Smokey and Temptations any day of the week, and I'm a happy camper. That's probably one of the reasons why Lance and I get along so well together. He's a true oldies fan too.

I turned on my cell phone when I crossed the Pennsylvania state line. I hadn't turned it on since I had left and I had fifteen voicemail messages. I connected my hands-free remote, turned off Marvin, figuring I'd holla at him later on. It wasn't like he would be going anywhere. The first three messages were from Rashan of course.

Message 1: "Yo, where you at? Holla at ya boy when you get this message."

Message 2: "I guess you ain't around. I hope you ain't sweating that shit that happened the other night. It's still all gravy between us. I just want you to get rid of that nucca so we can do this. I left Tawanna and the kids so you and me can hook up for real now. I need a place to lay low for a minute. Holla."

That asshlole must be on that chronic. No, for real. I knew that Rashan smoked that crap; he even tried to offer it to me a few times. I damn near smacked the stupid out of him. I don't do nobody's drugs. Later for that.

Now, he's telling me that he needs a place to stay. With who? Me? Wrong motherfucking answer. Did he not get the wake-up call when I put my steel to his chin? We are done and

78

BEWARE OF DOG!

ain't no other way about it. It's over and that's that.

I decided to skip Message 3 because it was my Daddy, trying to tell me about his latest golfing event.

Message 4: "Hey baby, where you been? I called you at home, but haven't heard from you. I hope everything is alright. Call me and let me know you're on point. I want to see you real soon," Lance stated.

I knew there was a reason why I was feeling Lance so much. He knew exactly how to handle me. Not too much attention, just the right amount of space and plenty of good loving.

Message 5: "Corie, it's Lisa. I hope you get this message I've tried beeping you because you didn't leave a number where I could reach you. Call me back. I can't stay all week. I'm not going to leave you hanging, but Vanita said she has things under control, but I don't want to leave here before I speak with you. I wish you would have left a number for me to call you or at least you would've kept your phone on. Call me as soon as you get this message."

My club in the hands of a person I don't trust that well. Oh hell naw. I hung up and immediately called my cousin Lisa on her cell phone.

"Where the hell have you been?" Lisa yelled into the phone. "What's wrong?" I asked, way past the beginning stages of worrying.

"It's cool. Carla came down with some type of stomach virus, so I need to get back to Wilmington and run my shit. I got one of my managers there now, but you know I ain't built on trusting a whole bunch of folks with my business."

"I feel you on that. I'm on my way back now. I should be there in about twenty-five minutes."

"Everything was cool here, as far as the money. I've got

everything written down," Lisa explained.

Slowly, my color began coming back. If I could trust anybody in this world with my club, Lisa was the one. I knew she would treat my business as if it were her own.

"Oh yeah, some dude keeps coming in here looking for you. I had to tell Jerry to put him out the other night. He said he was your man," Lisa said.

"Tall, cute, rough-neck lookin' dude?" I asked.

"Yeah, you know your type," Lisa stated sarcastically. I ain't never had it confirmed but it was rumored that my cousin and her business partner Carla, were How you doin'. In other words, they have their licker licenses—you know as in lesbians. I ain't mad at them. The way I see it, the more lesbians in the world, more men for me. So lick on.

"That's nobody but Rashan. What did he do for you to put him out?"

"He kept coming up in here asking—no demanding—to know where you were. Talking about he was going up to your office to chill and wait for you. I had to step to him. So Jerry just told him to roll out. The boy acted like he wanted to start some action up in here," Lisa stated.

"I gotta handle that situation when I get back."

"Please do. You want me to wait for you to get here?" Lisa asked.

"Naw, you go ahead. Thanks for everything. I'll call you later on tonight. Tell Carla I hope she feels better," I stated.

"Thanks, will do."

When I arrived back in Philly around 3:30 PM I went straight to the club. I was feeling really uneasy about things. I don't tell many people about my personal business, so if it gets out, than I'll know from where it came.

BEWARE OF DOG!

By now, you may be thinking that I'm a royal bitch. For the most part, you're right. I have a lot of issues that I'm still dealing with. Don't act as if your house is totally in order.

After I graduated from Fisk seven years ago, I returned to Philly to attend graduate school at Wharton. During my last year, in January, I found out that I was pregnant. I was seeing this guy named Jarvis. Of course Jarvis had the thug look, but he was definitely a brotha on the move. I mean this was a guy who had a scholarship to Wharton and I met him in the library of all places. We hit it off instantly.

I was truly digging him back then. Jarvis was probably one of the smartest men I've ever had the opportunity to meet. When I told him I was pregnant, he was real cool about the whole thing. Since we were both graduating in May, the baby didn't really interfere with our studies. I moved out of my apartment and moved in with Jarvis since he rented a small town house near the art museum. We both graduated with honors and things were going well. After graduation, I began trying to build my portfolio and searching for investors for my business venture. In August, I began having severe contractions and subsequently went into labor two months early, delivering a two-pound baby boy. He looked just like his mommy, even early on. We named him Tori. I stayed at that hospital day and night, just waiting to take my baby home. On my original due date, the worse thing that could have ever happened to me occurred: I lost my little baby. I'll be honest, a piece of me died too. I changed that day and haven't been the same since. Now, don't get me wrong, I've always been a little hardcore, but I know that this tough exterior is my shield against the world. Besides my parents, my girl, Troi was the only person who was truly there for me, not just physically, but spiritually, mentally, the whole nine yards.

BEWARE OF DOG!

After Tori's funeral, I left Jarvis. I moved in a small downtown apartment and have only seen him once.

One year after Tori's death, I opened the club. I had graduated on time and had managed to devote all of my waking moments to getting the club up and running. Jarvis walked in with his brother, Al, and just sat and stared at me all evening long. He kept trying to talk to me throughout the night, but I tried avoiding him at all costs. By the end of the night, his brother Al had left the club and Jarvis just sat there on the bar stool, nursing his drink, looking pitiful.

"Jarvis, what's happening, hon?"

"Sit and talk with me. I miss you so much."

"Come on now. Let me get you a ride home."

"I don't need a ride. I want you!" he stated.

"Come on. You're drunk. Let me get you home. Where are you staying these days?" I asked.

"I still live in the same house. I finally brought it."

"Good for you. Let me call you a cab. The address is 2743, right?" I asked.

"How easily we forget. It's only been a year. It's 2723," Jarvis stated.

"Oh, my bad. I'll be right back," I said, turning to call him a cab.

"Wait. I want to talk to you. Can we go somewhere and talk? Or you can come back to my place so we can be together?"

"That's not a good idea," I stated.

"Why?"

"Jarvis, I loved you. Part of me will always love you for what we had together. But, every time I look into your eyes, I see Tori's eyes. It just hurts too badly. Please, just go," I stated as I attempted to turn and walk away again.

BEWARE OF DOG!

"Don't do this to me. I can't eat, sleep or think about anything but you. To have lost Tori and then you, it's been too much to bear. Sometimes I feel like I can't go on. I need you, Corie," he said.

"Move on, Jarvis. I can't help you. I'm giving it my all just to get through the day. I can't be your rock and mine too. Talk to someone about it. Don't hold it in."

"You ain't shit. I can't believe you're going to turn your back on me like this," he stated.

"I just can't be there for you. Get over it," I said.

"You're going to get yours for this."

"I know you're not threatening me," I said.

"Can you just sit and talk with me?"

I've gotta go," I said, turning to leave him and to never look him in the eyes ever again. I just couldn't or else I would see Tori's soul. I walked upstairs and had a good, hearty cry then I moved on. I had to. In the days after Tori passed, I felt myself slipping mentally. I would hear a baby cry, and I'd break out in a deep sweat and hyperventilate. I saw a therapist for six months. Then, and only then, was I able to put those feelings away and move on. Jarvis was a constant reminder of the life that I needed to forget. I think that's why I don't want to get too close to any man, for fear of him wanting to get married, have children, and for what, to have it all wiped away again in a blink of an eye? No thanks. That's why this club is so important to me. In a lot of ways The Blue Nile has become the baby I lost. I vowed that I would guard my business with my life, the same way that I would have guarded my son's life had he still been here for me to see him grow.

I walked into the club and felt that this was where I truly belonged. I could tell Lisa was in the middle of cleaning because she had left everything on the counter. Actually, I was

BEWARE OF DOG!

a bit surprised that she left without putting the rags, the bucket, the ice…and when I looked closely, there was a huge stack of money on the counter. Suddenly, I realized something wasn't right. Then, under the door to the basement, I noticed smoke and then the fire alarm began blaring. The next thing I knew the sprinklers came on and I heard a distant cry for help. I picked up the phone and didn't hear a dial tone. I ran for the basement door and when I opened it, I saw Lisa tied up at the bottom of the steps. I tried to run to help her, but just then, I felt a large thump on my head. The next thing I knew, I heard a small child calling for me. It was Tori. "Mommy, come to me." My baby was reaching for me. The only thing to do was reach back, right?

BEWARE OF DOG!

"Rather than defeat your enemies, seek to transform them into allies."
—Author unknown

Chapter 8

Xavier

This job is becoming a little too stressful at times. Monday was my first day to report to Central Detectives. I had a murder-suicide case that was assigned to me and two senior detectives had just retired, which meant I received their entire caseload. The city had me ripping and running all over Philly, chasing leads and what-not and for once in my marriage, I didn't have time for anything other than Stacey and the kids. The flipside of things was, when I was at home, I was so tired that I didn't have time for Stacey and the kids.

Just when I didn't think my caseload could get any heavier, my supervisor threw even more work on my plate. But I'm a man, I don't complain, I just bite down on the bullet. I almost had some drama when I stopped calling my side honey, who's married. Now, don't get me wrong, I've been living by all of my concrete rules, but this situation happened without me knowing. You see, my side honey was having problems with her man, and things got so out of control that he left her. Who would have known this one was coming?

BEWARE OF DOG!

To make matters worse, she didn't even tell me she was having some issues at home. One day she calls me up and asks me to come over to her place. Now, I'm not crazy, so of course I said, hell no because that would be a violation of the rules. She starts explaining how her husband doesn't live there anymore and how it's okay if I come over to spend time with her while the kids were at school. Mind you, she and her husband have three kids. Anyway, I told her that I was really busy at work and that I couldn't get there. She started acting up, cursing me out, so I had to pull one of my better lines out. Now, you can use this line if you want. I told her, "You'd rather me run down there and like you a lot, than walk to you slowly and love you a lot." She gave me all of the space I needed after that. I made her think I was marinating this whole relationship thing, when in actuality, I was giving her time to get me out of her system, once and for all.

The writing was on the wall with that one, so I eased on out the picture and she eventually left me alone. In fact, I was getting tired of all of these women. It was time that I stepped off these women for a while. Concentrate on Stacey, the kids and me.

I was riding with my partner, Clinton, and he was telling me all about some drama that occurred in one of the police districts.

"Man, you hear about Earl and his issues?" Clinton asked.

"Naw, man, what happened?"

"You know that girl he met at that strip club over in Jersey, the one with the banging body that all the guys be trying to holla at?"

"You talking about Tamika?" I asked.

"I don't know her name. You know I don't go out like

BEWARE OF DOG!

that."

"Why, what's up with that?" I asked.

"Well, apparently Earl had a bachelor's party for his brother over at the Hyatt last month and things got out of hand, if you know what I mean," Clinton stated.

"Man, spit it out. What the hell happened?"

"This should be a wake-up call to all of you brothas out there helping to destroy the black family," Clinton rambled.

"Are you going to tell me or do I have to hear about it on Oprah? What happened?"

"Man, the word on the street is that after the party, Earl and two of his boys paid her an extra five hundred dollars to give them a private party. Everybody left and they supposedly pulled a train on her. Well, you know that Earl's wife is pregnant, and when she had some blood work done, it came back positive for HIV."

"What? Man, get the fuck out of here. Are you serious?" I asked in disbelief.

"That's the word. They said Earl tried to kill himself, that's why he's in the hospital. Didn't you hear he was in the hospital?" Clinton asked.

"Man, I've been on my grind, trying to get this overtime. Hell no. Did the other two boys get tested?" I asked.

"Yup, and they both came back positive too."

"Man, how the hell you know all of this?" I asked.

"Let's just say, that I know for a fact that this ain't no lie. This was confirmed, almost by the doctor himself."

"I was supposed to go to that bachelor's party. Not that I would have participated in that kind of crap."

"You sure? You never know what you might do when you're drinking and feeling the vibe," Clinton stated.

"Naw, man. There ain't that much desperation in the

world," I responded.

"Just be sure, man. This AIDS thing is wiping us out left and right, especially our women of color. Can you imagine what must be going through Earl's mind knowing that he gave his wife HIV and possibly his unborn child?" Clinton asked.

"That's wild. I've been chilling lately. I think God may be trying to tell me something. I think I better lay low."

"That's what I've been trying to tell you," Clinton stated.

"Don't start preaching man."

That conversation with Clinton really shook me up for a few days. But, I had to know if what he told me was true. If there's one thing in this world that I'm petrified of, that's contracting AIDS. Besides that, the girl who gave the guys AIDS tried to give me some rhythm before. Thankfully, I can honestly say that I didn't mess around with her. I'm not into women that strip for a living. That doesn't turn me on. But, the fact that I was supposed to go to that bachelor's party and she would have been coming on to me and there's no telling what I would've done if I had a few drinks in me. I might have let her at least suck my dick and that alone can get you sick with HIV or herpes or something. I mean, it's not like I would have put a condom on, more than likely.

I was going to call up to Temple Hospital, because that's where I heard Earl was admitted to, but I decided to go up there personally. I badged my way up to his room and when I walked in, I knew right then and there that I had to change my ways. The look in Earl's eyes said it all. I've never seen a grown man cry the way he did. I never even got a word out of my mouth. I guess he knew that everyone else knew and the shame was too much for him to handle. I looked at him with his wrists bandaged and his eyes were damn near swollen shut. If I could have killed him to put him out of his misery I would have. He

BEWARE OF DOG!

just looked pathetic. Finally, he stopped crying and there was a silence in the air that was almost sickening.

"Earl, if I can do anything for you, you know that I'll do it."

"Man, make sure you never, ever fuck with another woman without using a condom. That's what you can do for me."

" 'Nough said, man. How's your wife doing?"

"She lost the baby. I guess the stress alone did it. Man, I feel like shit. In a way, I'm glad she lost it. I could never look that baby in the eyes, knowing because I was careless, his or her life would have been shortened. Man, I'm hurting inside. I'd kill myself a hundred times if I thought I could right this wrong," Earl said.

There was nothing that I could say. All I know is that God puts these situations before us, and you either learn from them or you don't. I knew that I had to learn from my mistakes and Earl's. I had a lot of growing up to do, and I had to be more conscious of the decisions I made. I made a vow to myself, that I hoped and prayed I could keep. I promised to be faithful to my marriage. It was a vow I could keep, right?

BEWARE OF DOG!

**"There are no true friendships without conflict."
—Zen Buddah**

Chapter 9

Troi

I awakened on Thursday morning, ready to head home. It was the day before my last one in New York City, and although I had a great time, almost committing a grave sin, I was now ready to go home and face the music. I had a dream about Gavin in the middle of the night, and it seemed so real.

I awakened to his huge arms wrapped around me, and I slowly began the huge task of removing his large biceps from my torso. He awakened just as I was getting dressed.

"Where are you going, baby? I was going to order breakfast for us."

"I need to get back to my room. I have some calls to make to my office before the early morning rush."

"Come on, get back in this bed. Do you have to go to your seminar this morning? I wanna make love to you over and over," Gavin said, patting the mattress.

"Uh, I can't. I really need to get to work," I stated.

"When can I see you again? Tonight?" he asked.

"I don't think we should see each other again."

"What?"

90

BEWARE OF DOG!

"You heard me. What we had happened. It's time to move on," I said.

"Oh, it's like that. Huh? I thought this was going to be a little more than just a casual fling on the road."

"What gave you that impression? I wanted to fuck and that's what we did. Don't start catching feelings all of a sudden."

"It's not even like that. Calm down. I like you, and I want to see you again."

"Listen, you're married and I'm engaged. Let's leave it that way. What could possibly ever come of this? You're not leaving your wife and I'm not leaving my fiancé. Let what was, be just that."

"You're hardcore."

"No, I'm not. Men just can't take it when women flip the script."

"It's cool, babe. I just thought when I was nearby or you were in my area, we could kick it. You know, no strings attached."

"I have your business card. I'll call you."

"Let me lick you all over again."

In the dream, I walked past him, dropping my towel to the floor and headed for the shower. As I was nearing the daunting task of removing all of the suds from my breasts, Gavin walks in with his Greek like body. He drops to his knees and places my foot high up on the soap dish. He sticks his long, warm tongue inside of me, and I let out a loud moan. Just as I'm nearing a damn orgasm, you guessed it, the phone rings. It's the wake-up call that I dreaded. Just like that, no more dream.

I willed myself out of bed and jumped in the shower, attempting to wash some of the sinful thoughts off me. I peeked

in on Corie and she was sound asleep. Since I was leaving the following morning, I packed up most of my belongings, laying out only the items I would need for my last night in New York. After I packed, I quickly dressed and headed downstairs to meet Jennifer in the lobby. I checked in on Corie before I left and she was still sound asleep.

My day at the seminar wasn't so bad. It was Thursday, and I gave my presentation without many problems, other than the fact that I was a little anxious to get back home.

"Great job, Troi. Thanks for giving that presentation at the last minute. I'm glad everything worked out," Jennifer stated.

"No problem. Glad to be of assistance," I responded.

"Are we still on for this afternoon?" Jennifer asked, referring to our shopping trip with Corie.

"I don't know. Let me call her on my cell," I said.

I retrieved my phone from my Burberry attaché briefcase and noticed that I had eight missed calls and three voice mail messages.

Message 1: "Troi, I need you to call me ASAP. There's been an emergency with Corie. Call me." It was Malcolm, who was near frantic. I was slightly confused because Corie was with me in New York. Knowing Malcolm, he was probably lying again.

Message 2: "Troi, where the hell are you? I hate when you don't answer your phone. Call me the minute you get this message," Malcolm stated.

Message 3: "Troi, baby. Call me, baby. It's Auntie Simms. I don't know if you've spoken to Malcolm, but Corie is in the hospital. Call me on my cell phone when you get this message." It was Corie's mom, my godmother, Aunt June. Now, I knew that something was terribly wrong.

BEWARE OF DOG!

I called Aunt June and she answered in her heavy Guyanese accent, on the first ring.

"Troi, baby, where are you?" Aunt June asked.

"Auntie, I'm in New York. What happened?" I asked.

"We don't know, yet. The police are here asking us a million questions. Someone, assaulted Corie and Lisa at the club. Lisa's in a coma and Corie's unconscious," Aunt June stated.

"What? Corie was with me here in New York. She must have left this morning. I'm on my way. Is Corie alright?" I asked.

"She's got a concussion, but she'll be fine. It's Lisa that's not doing so well. She was bound and gagged and she's suffering from smoke inhalation," Aunt June explained.

"My God. Who would do a thing like this?" I asked.

"You know the world has some crazy folks in it. I've gotta run. I just walked outside to get some fresh air. I need to get back in there to see if the doctors have any new information. When can you get here?" Aunt June asked.

"I'll be there in about two hours. I'm taking the first train out of here. I'll see you later, Auntie," I stated, hanging up the phone.

"I've got to go. Corie's in the hospital." I turned to Jennifer.

"Omigod! Go, go."

I grabbed a taxi and had the driver arrive to the hotel in record time to retrieve my belongings. Good thing I had packed up my clothes earlier that morning. I grabbed my things and raced across the street to Penn Station to get the first thing smoking out of New York. Thankfully, I was catching all kinds of the breaks because boarding time was only fifteen minutes away.

BEWARE OF DOG!

It seemed as if the train crawled to Thirtieth Street Station. I tried calling Malcolm several times on his cell phone, but all I got was his voicemail. Now, it was my turn to be pissed. What a time to have his phone turned off. As soon as the train stopped, I ran upstairs and literally pushed this woman out of the door to get into the cab. I'd have to ask for repentance at a later date. I arrived to Hahnaman Hospital in five minutes. Thankfully, the train station wasn't that far from the hospital.

When I arrived to the lobby, I was greeted by Aunt June and Uncle Craig, Corie's parents and Lisa's girlfriend Carla. Aunt June caught me up to speed. She was talking a mile a minute in her heavy accent, and I could barely keep up. Both Corie's and my parents are from Guyana, and although I can hang with the best of them in our native dialect, it took a few seconds for each of Aunt June's words to register, since she was so wound up. As it turned out, Corie had regained consciousness, but she was still being interviewed by the detectives, so we had to wait to see her.

Lisa, on the other hand, wasn't doing so well. She inhaled a lot of smoke and was still in a coma. Poor Carla. Lisa's live-in roommate looked like she wanted to just curl up and die. On top of all of that, she was just recuperating from some sort of stomach virus and she looked like hell.

When the detective came out of Corie's room, he began walking over to us I nearly fell over when I realized it was Xavier. The last time I had seen him was briefly in my office when he came in and wanted advice on family services. Xavier still looked good and still had the nicest eyes I'd ever seen on a man.

"Ma'am, your daughter would like to see you two now, The nurse said it was okay for you to go in," Xavier said.

BEWARE OF DOG!

"Thanks, Detective DeVoe," Aunt June responded.

He looked at me and then came over and gave me a hug.

"Troi, good to see you. Sorry it had to be under these circumstances. What are you doing here?" Xavier stated.

"Corie. She's my best friend," I said.

"Wow, small world," he stated.

"Yeah. She and I are like sisters. You could say I'm a part of the family," I said.

"Well, I'll need to speak with you too. You may be able to shed some light on the case," he said.

"Anything at all."

"You have a few minutes?"

"Sure." Xavier led me to the cafeteria, and I felt horrible leaving Carla behind. She looked so dazed that I'm sure she didn't even notice that I was gone.

Xavier asked me so many questions that my head began spinning. What was supposed to be a few minutes turned into almost an hour. I told him all about Rashan and how he threatened Corie and how she was in New York with me and the next thing I know I'm getting called on my cell phone about Corie and Lisa being assaulted. I just felt so helpless to Corie. My best friend in the entire world was laying up in a hospital, and there was absolutely nothing that I could do to help her.

"If you think of anything or anyone that would want to hurt Ms. Simms, please give me a call," Xavier stated.

"Honestly, in your professional opinion, off the record of course, what do you think so far?" I asked.

"It's way too early to tell, but my professional hunch tells me someone wants your friend dead or seriously hurt. I talked to her about getting a bodyguard or carrying a firearm. Thankfully, she had a gun registered in her name, but it doesn't do any good when someone sneaks up on you," he stated.

95

BEWARE OF DOG!

"What can I do to help?" I asked.

"If you think of anything that could help me solve this case, call me. The best thing you can do for her is to keep your eyes and ears open. Someone's watching her, and you may be able to see or hear things that she's not seeing. Call me. I hope and pray your friend feels better," Xavier stated, handing me a business card, complete with his office and cellular phone numbers.

Xavier excused himself. I sat there in a trance for a few moments. How could this be happening? I knew that it was that damn Rashan. I told Corie time and time again to stop messing with these thugged-out rugged guys. They don't make men like they used to. These thugs nowadays will bash your head wide open and won't think twice about it. No damn respect for their own mama let alone the woman they're dealing with. Between the information that Corie gave Xavier and what I told him, there was no doubt in my mind that they'd have that Rashan character in jail in no time.

I sat there twirling Xavier's business card in my hands, reminiscing. When Xavier came into my office, back when he was seeking a divorce lawyer, he looked much different than the first time that I had met him. He was decked out in a pair of Sean John jeans, Sean John mock turtleneck, and his curly hair was neatly trimmed in a mini afro. I'm not going to lie and tell you that I wasn't extremely impressed with his good looks. You know, the type of man who can be found hosting a nightly BET special or something. But, when I'm on the job, I'm strictly professional and I was all deeply in love with Malcolm at the time anyway. Speaking of which, where the hell was he? I pulled out my cell phone and just as I was about to call him, a nurse walked up and told me about the hospital's no cell phone policy. I started to argue with her, but then I remembered that

BEWARE OF DOG!

those rules were in place for a reason and my best friend and her cousin were laying up in the hospital, for heaven's sake. I decided to call Malcolm from a pay phone instead. I let it ring three times before Malcolm answered all flabbergasted, yet again.

"Stop calling here, I'm going to get your fucking money," Malcolm screamed into the receiver.

"What? What the hell are you talking about?" I asked.

"What? Who's this?" Malcolm replied.

"It's your fucking fiancé. Malcolm, what the hell are you doing?"

"Oh shit. I thought it was Keith. I owe him some money from a football game we bet on last week," Malcolm stated.

"Football? Malcolm, I know I don't know a lot about sports but, isn't this the summertime? What football game could you possibly be betting Keith with in the summer? " I asked.

"Naw, a few of the brahs got together and played some football in Fairmount Park last week. That's what I'm talking about."

"Whatever. Anyway, I got your message. What's the emergency?" I asked, figuring I'd play dumb since Malcolm was obviously lying and hiding something from me.

"I got a call from Aunt June that Corie was in the hospital. I figured you'd want to know."

"Hospital! What's wrong?" I asked, all fake shocked and what-not. I was involved in the drama club in high school.

"Corie got attacked or something. You know how Aunt June gets all worked up and starts speaking in tongues or whatever it is y'all be speaking," Malcolm stated.

"Don't make fun of my people. That shit funny," I said,

97

BEWARE OF DOG!

adding my Guyanese accent to let him know I meant business.

"Oh, I forgot. Why you does that? Isn't that how you say it?" Malcolm replied, ignoring my warning.

"You think that's funny? My best friend is laid up in the fucking hospital and you're making jokes."

"What I did?" Malcolm replied, still continuing with his damn jokey jokes. I simply said nothing, hanging up in his ear. I didn't know what had gotten into my fiancé but he was acting awfully strange and so help me I was going to get to the bottom of it.

I went back upstairs and told Aunt June and Uncle Craig that I was heading home. Corie was asleep and they weren't allowing any visitors to see her anyway. Carla was still in a trance and by that time other family members had come up to the hospital for moral support. As far as Malcolm knew, I was still in New York. Whatever happened when I arrived home, I prayed I wouldn't be sitting in someone's jail for the rest of my life. I'm way too cute to be Big Bertha's bitch.

The minute I got outside, my phone rang. It was Jennifer.

"How are you? How's Corie doing?" Jennifer asked, shooting questions at me a mile per minute.

"She'll be fine. She has a concussion, but she'll live. Her cousin, who was running her club, wasn't so lucky. She has smoke inhalation and she's in a coma," I responded.

"Omigod. That's horrible. Do they know who did it?" Jenn asked.

"They have a few leads but they haven't arrested the guy I think is behind it."

"I hope they hang the bastard."

"Me too."

"Listen, Gavin asked me where you were and I told him

BEWARE OF DOG!

you had an emergency. I hope you don't mind, but I gave him your cell phone number," Jennifer stated.

"You did what!"

"I didn't think you'd mind. You guys seemed to have hit it off all week. I hope you're not mad at me."

"I just wished you would have asked me first. Now I have to try and dodge his damn calls."

"If it's any consolation, he seemed pretty upset that you left suddenly. I told him you had an emergency, and he was very concerned."

"Really now? Listen, I wish I could chitchat, but I've got some fish to fry," I stated.

"You're cooking with all that's going on?"

"It's a saying. I've got shit to do. Can you hear me now? Good!"

"Calm down, I'm not up on all of my slang. Alright. Call me if I can do anything for you. And again, I apologize for giving Gavin your number," Jennifer stated sincerely.

"Alright. I'll holla at you later in the week," I said.

"Don't do that. I thought you weren't mad," Jennifer teased before she hung up the phone.

I tried and tried to hail a taxi out in front of Hahnaman, but for some odd reason, the cabs were all full. Just when I thought I was going to have to catch a dreaded Septa bus, Xavier pulled out of the parking lot and pulled in front of the curb. "How far are you going?"

"I live at Twenty-second and Spruce," I said.

"Climb in. Now you see what the brothas have to go through to catch a taxi in the city."

"Yeah, we should start a class action suit. I could file for all of you. Why don't you have a partner?" I asked.

"I do, but I figured I could handle this portion of the

99

BEWARE OF DOG!

investigation by coming out to the hospital."

"I can't wait for you guys to catch that bastard who did this," I said.

"We'll get whoever did this. You have my word on it. Listen, you wanna go grab a cup of coffee or something? It's no sense in you going home when you're visibly upset."

"You know, that's not a bad idea," I responded.

"I know this diner on Twelfth and Walnut. They have great roast beef, if you're hungry. Besides, you can tell me more about Ms. Simms and maybe that can shed some light on her case."

"Now you sound as if you're trying to justify us grabbing a bite to eat," I said.

" I just don't want you to feel uncomfortable," Xavier stated.

"Xavier, how long have you been with the police department?" I asked.

"I've been with the department for seven years," he responded. "You married?"

"I guess you could call it that," I replied.

"Uh-oh. Is the divorce lawyer in need of her own services?"

"No, I'm getting married in just six months, or at least I'm supposed to. But, check with me in an hour and all that might be changing," I responded.

"Oh, you've got to go home to deal with some issues?" he asked.

"You don't know the half of it."

"So, I guess it's fair to say that you're royally pissed off with your fiancé?"

"I don't discuss my problems with old boyfriends and clients. That's a conflict of interest."

BEWARE OF DOG!

"Remember, I'm no client and if I would've been your boyfriend, you'd know it. I worked things out with my wife."

"Good for you," I said sarcastically.

"I just figured I'd offer a supportive ear. From one friend to another. I know marriage can be hard sometimes, but then again, no one has to tell you that," he stated.

"How long have you been married?" I asked.

"Forever," he responded.

"That's not exactly answering my question," I said.

"Forever. I'm married forever. Some people try to quantify marriage with a number, as if to reduce its ideology. When I married my wife it was forever. We've had our ups and downs, but we're trying to hang on in there now."

"If marriage is forever than why did you feel a need to come see me?"

"Because I can be an asshole at times. I haven't always been faithful. That doesn't mean that I don't love my wife, but I guess I have a lot of growing to do."

"How is it that we find ourselves in these situations sometimes? I mean, I just don't understand how one person can make you extremely happy one minute and you can love that person with all of your heart and soul and then that very same person is the one who you can come to despise," I said.

"It's easy. It doesn't take very much for some people to lose interest. You see, lots of people cheat or experiment—call it what you like, but it's all the same. Some men and women cheat when they get bored with the same person day in and day out, some people cheat when they're not being satisfied, either emotionally and or physically and some people simply don't have a conscience at all and it's merely about the physical. That's my opinion," Xavier stated.

"Let me ask you an honest question. Why did you cheat

BEWARE
OF
DOG!

on your wife?" I asked.

"I got married young. That's no excuse for my behavior, but I was only twenty-two when I got married. I hadn't seen a lot of the world when I began meeting women of all shapes, sizes and colors, and I just had this overpowering urge to bed as many women as I could. My wife and I used to have a good time but there was something lacking. Besides that, meeting women day in and day out on this job doesn't help matters," I said.

"What's your story now?" I asked.

"Right now, I'm living my life one day at a time. I can't promise what I won't ever cheat again. Hell, I'd be foolish to do that. To me, one should never say never. You don't know what you'd do in a particular situation. But, a good friend of mine just gave his wife AIDS as a result of infidelity and it's a wake-up call that I'm listening to loud and clear," he said.

"Sorry to hear that about your friends. AIDS is a very real and tragic problem for our society, especially for black women. The statistics are alarmingly high for us. But, you're right. There are things that I've done that I'm not particularly proud of, and I've said that I wouldn't do a lot of things, ever, and yet I've found myself doing those exact same things that I said I'd never, ever do," I stated quietly.

We continued to travel in silence as we headed over to the diner. Xavier was a complete gentleman throughout the evening, not at all what I expected. I guess I had him all wrong. Although he was professional, it was something about his eyes that told me he was still missing something substantial in his marriage. I knew it all too well because I had the same miserable look in my eyes.

After two cups of coffee and a turkey special later, I decided that I needed to get home to take care of business.

BEWARE OF DOG!

Xavier gave me a ride home and I promised him that I'd be in touch. He was a great listener, but then again, I've never met a cop who wasn't—it's their job to listen. I felt as if I'd known him for years.

When we pulled up to my town house, I instantly knew there was going to be some trouble. Don't ask me how, but I just felt it in my bones. I played it real cool, 'cause I didn't want Xavier to know all of my business. As I opened the door, I turned and waved good bye. Before I even opened the door, I heard the Isley Brothers blaring over the PA system in the house. I calmly walked up the stairs and found Malcolm in the master bedroom with his back to the door on the phone, sitting on the bed. He must have heard me because he said something under his breath and then hung up the phone.

"What are you doing here?" he asked.

"I happen to live here or did you forget? Who were you talking to on the phone?" I asked.

"That was Louie from New York. You know that record exec I've been trying to reach? We had to go over some figures."

"You've been going over a lot of figures lately. Anything you want to share with me?"

"Naw. You know I don't like to talk about the business stuff with you. How's Corie doing?" he asked, trying to change the subject.

"She's fine. I just left the hospital. Her parents are there. I was sure that I'd see you up there. Have you been to see her yet?"

"Naw. I didn't think there was a point. You know I hate hospitals."

"Um-hmm," I said, turning to get as far away from him as possible.

BEWARE OF DOG!

"What's your problem? Come here," he said, grabbing my arm.

"Don't man-handle me. Get off me." I said, pulling my arm away from him.

"Come here. You're my woman. I missed you. Can't I touch my fiancé when I want to?" he asked, forcefully grabbing me around the waist.

"Malcolm, have you been drinking?"

"So what if I have? You're not my fucking mother. I'm tired of your ass thinking you know so much. You have way too much mouth. Since you've got so much mouth, why don't you put your mouth on this!" he said, grabbing his crotch.

"Fuck you, Malcolm," I said as I turned to head for the bathroom.

I don't know why I said that because he went ballistic. He turned me around by pulling my right shoulder. He picked me up and threw me on the bed. He straddled me and then took both of my hands in one of his, restraining mine to the bed.

He placed a wet, sloppy kiss on my mouth, and I began to become scared and slightly aroused at the same time. I knew in my heart that Malcolm would never hurt me, but there was a look in his eyes that was frighteningly different.

"I'm going to fuck you until you pass out."

"Malcolm, you're drunk, honey. Get off me."

"Shut up and just take this big dick," he said, unfastening his pants and pulling out his small, limp penis. With his free hand, Malcolm pulled up my dress as I tried to wiggle free. He then shifted my thong and fumbled with his penis to gain an erection.

"Get off of me, Malcolm. Now!" I demanded.

"Shut up. You know you love this big dick," Malcolm repeated. "Tell me it's the biggest dick you've ever seen."

BEWARE OF DOG!

"We both know that you're not related to any Mandingo warriors, Malcolm. Now get the hell off me before you do something that you'll regret," I warned.

"What the hell do you mean? You know I'm packing," Malcolm stated.

"Sweetheart, you and I both know that you're only three and-a-half inches and thirty seconds long on a good day. Now gather your limp noodle and get the hell off me," I demanded.

"Fuck you, Troi," he said, releasing me from his powerful grip and walking into the master bathroom, slamming the door.

I was furious. Malcolm had never treated me so harshly. I didn't know what the hell had gotten into him but things were going to have to change. It wasn't like our sex life was great. Malcolm was only good for one thing and that was pleasing me with his mouth. If he didn't have that going for him he'd be a total waste. Malcolm should have been nicknamed Tiny Tim. It was never really a problem in the past, but lately he just didn't do it for me, sexually. I mean how much can you really please a woman in all of thirty seconds flat? If I didn't get mine then I was shit out of luck. Whenever I would complain, Malcolm just kept insisting that he could please me anally, but I just wasn't it to that. I grabbed my handbag and raced to get as far away from Malcolm as humanly possible.

I guess it was safe to say that the honeymoon was officially over, before it even got started, right?

"I'd love to love you, but I'd hate to hate you."
—Natosha Gale Lewis, Author

Chapter 10

Xavier

Okay, my plans to remain faithful were going pretty well so far. I passed the ultimate test when I had I grabbed a bite to eat with Troi. I was so proud of myself for not coming on to her, but then it really wasn't that much of a challenge. Troi was different. She was definitely not the type of woman I'd want to treat with any form of disrespect. To step to her on a creepin' level would have been just that. I had way too much respect for her to do that. That's how I knew that I had evolved. I had taken Troi out to get a platonic cup of coffee and a bite to eat. No harm. Yeah, she was more gorgeous than I remembered, but I've seen beautiful women before and a pretty face just ain't enough anymore. There's got to be some sort of chemistry there. With Troi, although she and I hit it off as if we had been seeing each other for a lifetime, I just felt a need to take a step back. It was the type of feeling that I wanted in my wife. Troi evoked something in me that made we want to be a better man. We talked about everything from the ghetto to the White House, and for once a woman challenged what I said. I remember she answered the one question that I throw out to quite a few

BEWARE OF DOG!

people, but rarely can many folks answer it.

"Troi, if you had ten dollars to feed you and your family for three days, what would you buy to survive?"

"Alright, let me think for a moment."

"Take your time," I said.

"Okay, I've got it. I'd buy two pounds of potatoes, a bag of rice, a box of oatmeal and a loaf of bread," Troi stated.

I'm not going to lie, at that very moment I had a newfound respect for Troi because I realized how smart she was. I saw her in a completely different light, and I wanted nothing more than to reach out, scoop her up in my arms and kiss her until the sun came up. I know, I know, that was really corny, but that question means a lot to me. To be able to answer it tells me that a person is resourceful. If you can find your way out of a situation like that then a person can handle almost anything. I asked Stacey that very same question, and she told me that she'd buy some chicken. Try eating just poultry for one day and see if your ass ain't damn near starving. You need starch to fill you up. I tell you, when Stacey told me that I knew that I always had to be the one who looked out for our family because when it comes down to it, we couldn't survive off her logic.

After we had stayed at the restaurant for damn near two hours I decided that I really needed to get home. After all I was trying to walk the straight and narrow and although I was feeling the vibe that Troi and I obviously had, I wasn't going down that road. I dropped Troi off and, I headed home.

When I got there Stacey and the kids were asleep. I quickly undressed and showered and got in the bed with Stacey. I was horny as hell, and I needed a little loving from my wife. If I had to be honest with myself I knew that having dinner with Troi made me have a mental orgasm and I couldn't get Troi off

BEWARE OF DOG!

my mind. I could make love to Troi's mind every day of the week and she turned me on like I had never been aroused before.

I don't know what Stacey and I have. I think that Stacey is still pretty, but she could stand to gain a few pounds or at least tighten up what she has going on for herself. The best compliment that I could give Stacey is that she's an awesome cook. Other than that, we don't have much in common. To put it mildly, I'm bored. Stacey is the most boring person in the bed that I've ever encountered. She just lays there, never moving one muscle in her body. The only position for us in the basic missionary one. No foreplay needed, because there are many things that Stacey just doesn't do. No oral sex, no fingers, no nothing. If it ain't kissing on the lips, Stacey ain't having it! One night, a few years ago, I was watching this porno movie down in the basement. I was horny like you wouldn't believe. I turned that damn TV off and marched my ass right on up there to go for mine. Stacey was sound asleep, snoring and all. I just looked at her sleeping and she was out. You know, laying on her back, one leg cocked to the side and her nightgown was slightly raised. I pulled her panties over and placed my warm mouth over her vagina. She smelled so clean and fresh and I damn near lost control. Stacey started moaning and groaning and even started thrusting her hips. Oh, it was about to be on, or so I thought. Stacey suddenly stopped and woke up. "What the hell are you doing? Stop that now!" she yelled.

"What the hell are you talking about? You were enjoying it. Just go with the flow. Let me make you feel good," I pleaded.

"Xay, just stop it. I don't want to be bothered. Can't you get that through your greasy head?" she asked.

"Stacey, I'm a man and I have needs. I just don't want

BEWARE OF DOG!

to climb on top and have my way with you, but that's how you make me feel. Like I'm having sex with a damn farm animal. Do you even enjoy sex?" I asked.

"Xay, I was always brought up to believe that sex is for the man. To be honest with you I can't say that I enjoy it. I just don't see the hype," she explained.

"Let me show you the hype, baby. You see how you were feeling just a few minutes ago? Imagine that times one hundred."

"I can't. I just can't!" she stated as she got out of the bed and went into the bathroom, locking the door.

Over the next few years, I'd tried to sneak in a little action, while Stacey was asleep. Hell, one night I tried to get her a little buzzed, but Stacey wasn't having it. So, there I was, left unfulfilled by a woman that I loved for so many reasons outside of sex, but then again, sex is a huge part of a marriage and hell, I've got needs that have to be met. Have you ever been in a relationship and although you love that person and you've built a life with her and you may even have kids together, you have a beautiful home, the white picket fence and all, and Lord knows you should be content, but you're just not happy? Is that being selfish? Is life meant to be that way? I certainly don't think so. I guess that's why I creep out on Stacey. It's not that I don't love her and what-not, but I guess I'm just not being fulfilled, and I'm looking for fulfillment with all of these other women. I just need more. I know I sound like a real-live asshole but I have to be true to me. If not me, who?

Anyway, I got in the bed with Stacey and I began rubbing and kissing over her neck. It used to be a time when I could kiss Stacey on the right side of her neck and she would give me a little bit more response than she normally does, but this time, like so many times before, she just laid there. I knew

BEWARE
OF
DOG!

that she was awake because she let out this long sigh, as if I was annoying her yet again. Now, normally, I just climb up on Stacey, give her about fifty good pumps and then I'm done. Hell, Courtney Vance needs to have a contract out on me because Angela Bassett is all up in my day dreams. But this time I guess Courtney stole his wife away for the night because not even my girl could bring any drive out of me. I promised myself when I heard Stacey sigh from me touching her that it was the last time that I would touch my wife in that way. Do you know what that does to man's self-esteem? Do you know that in the twelve years that Stacey and I have been married that she's never, ever, ever approached me for sex or has never even nuzzled up to me in the middle of the night. Shit, I like to be held too.

I suddenly turned over on my side and after a few minutes Stacey was lightly snoring. I guess she was happy that she didn't have to oblige me. I got up and went downstairs to look at a porno. Hell, since I couldn't make love to my wife, five-finger Billy was my main man. Off to another night of beating my meat.

I went downstairs and popped in a DVD that my man Kevin had loaned me. I tried and tried to get into the porno but Russell the Love Muscle just wasn't responding. I was relieved when my work cell phone rang.

"This is Detective DeVoe."

"Xay, it's me Troi," she stated.

"What's up, Troi? Can't get enough of me, huh? What's goin' on?"

"The reason I called is someone broke into Corie's home. I'm here now and they basically wrecked the place," she explained.

"Have you touched anything?" I asked.

BEWARE OF DOG!

"No. I left everything the way it was and I'm calling you from my cell phone," she explained.

"What are you doing there? I dropped you off at your house a while ago," I inquired.

"I got into a fight with Malcolm. But, I'm not trying to get into all of that. Can you come over?" she asked.

"Where are you now?" I asked.

"I'm in my car. I'm parked in Corie's garage," she explained.

"Pull out onto the street. I'll send a patrol car over there to make sure no one is still in the house."

"Thanks, Xavier."

"I'll see you in a few," I said before hanging up and heading upstairs to take a quick cold shower.

I left Stacey a note, telling her that I had to go out on business but I knew from how she was acting lately that she couldn't possibly care where I was going.

When I arrived, the patrol car was out front and the police officer was making his report. No one was found in the house. Except for a broken window in the dining room, some papers strewn about and some overturned furniture; everything was pretty much in order, from what I could tell. Of course I couldn't tell what had been stolen, but from the looks of things, the perps who had entered the premises, knew the victim. The first mistake the perp made was to break the window. The glass was found outside, but this was probably to just throw us off. Once the police officer left, Troi began the task of putting things back in their proper place.

"Here, let me help you with that," I said as Troi attempted to return a four-foot lamp in an upright position.

"Thanks. I can't believe all of this drama is happening."

"Let's go over here and sit down," I said, heading over

BEWARE OF DOG!

to the dining room table.

Troi explained how she had gone home and had gotten into an argument with her fiancé and how he began screaming at her at the top of his lungs.

As the tears came to her eyes and she continued to tell me how enraged he looked and how before she left for New York he had called her every name other than the child of God, I grew angrier and angrier. I could feel the veins bulging out of the side of my neck. In the next moment, I don't know what came over me, but I reached out and took Troi in my arms and held her there where she began sobbing. I could have held her for all of eternity. If I had to be honest with myself, it was the first time in my life I felt my heart skip a beat for a woman.

At first, Troi didn't hold on to me in return, but then she put her arms around my waist and didn't seem to want to let go either. Finally, she calmed down and looked up at me with those big brown eyes. She didn't say a word but her eyes told it all. She just wanted to be loved. I knew that what Stacey and I had was not real love, but just two people who did what they had to do for society's sake, holding on to a bad marriage because we had been together for twelve years and had two children.

I sat Troi down on the couch and she continued crying. I got up to get her a glass of water but she pulled me back down to sit with her. She grabbed the back of my neck and pulled my lips to hers, followed by a delicate kiss on the lips. At first, I was in shock. Never would I have pegged Troi for the type of woman to be so forward, especially since she was almost married. Aside from all of that, that's a move I'd normally make, and here this woman was seducing me and since I never get any kind of love like that at home, it was a welcome surprise. I tried standing because I just didn't feel right about

BEWARE OF DOG!

this. Something told me that Troi was different from what I remembered. This was no wam-bam-thank-you-ma'am situation. I was feeling this woman, and that was dangerous, especially since I have rules and I was trying to make good on that vow with my marriage. But after tonight's episode with Stacey, how long was my marriage going to last anyway, if I had vowed not to touch Stacey again since it was unwelcomed? I was in charge for a change. Troi whispered in my ear, "No strings attached. I just need to be wanted right now. Fuck me."

Well, you know that did it for me. I was hooked. I stood us up and grabbed her around her waist. I led her over to the wall and turned her around. I lifted her tank top and began kissing her along her soft, beautiful body, allowing my tongue to travel from her earlobe to the small of her back. I took my hand and began massaging her firm breasts. I kissed her earlobe, and I heard her make a soft moan. I knew right then and there I had her where I wanted her, or was it the other way around? To hear Troi, I was making her feel absolutely wonderful, and it was driving each motion farther and farther. Troi then took control of the situation and pushed me to the wall. She began lifting my shirt and kissing me on my chest and then she fell to her knees and began unfastening my pants, allowing them to drop to the floor. At first she was teasing me, kissing me all over my thighs and around my penis. She took each of my balls and placed them in her mouth. Suddenly, I felt her warm mouth on my penis, and I damn near exploded right then and there, but I wasn't going out like that. Not to compare or anything, but you know Stacey has never performed oral sex on me. Never! Troi definitely knew what she was doing, and it seemed as if she was hell bent on doing nothing but pleasing me.

Troi led me past the kitchen to a large bedroom on the

first floor. When we got inside, I laid her on the bed and began removing her clothes completely. I marveled at the sight of her body and began kissing every inch of her. I wanted nothing more than to please every nook and cranny of her beautiful body. I gently opened her legs and placed each of her feet on my shoulders and set in to literally drink all of her sweet-tasting juices that oozed from her body. She squirmed and moaned and groaned, and every twist and grunt that she gave it drove me further toward pleasing her. Finally, she began screaming, "I'm cumming, I'm cumming," as we both collapsed on the bed in utter bliss.

Troi then surprised me by going in the nightstand to retrieve a female condom.

"Troi, I don't want to fuck you. I know this sounds like a line, but I want to make love to you," I whispered in her ear.

A single tear escaped from her eye, and I kissed it away before I entered her, our eyes locked, and we both knew there was no turning back. It was something that we both wanted and yet, I can only speak for myself when I say this was just going to be more than a casual fling. I was feeling Troi since I had first laid eyes on her, and if she permitted me I wanted to be in her life from now on. I still hesitated and then she grabbed the back of my neck and pulled me in for a deep, passionate kiss. She placed her legs around my back and guided me inside the warmth of her body. She was so warm and tight; it felt like a wet leather glove. The entire experience, all night long, was unbelievable. I brought out stamina in myself that I never knew existed, and Troi was right along with me. The sad part about the whole thing is that Stacey never crossed my mind because Troi was too busy blowing it. I knew what we had done wasn't right, but it damn sure felt okay. We fell asleep in each other's arms and everything just seemed so right. I didn't have to

BEWARE
OF
DOG!

worry about calling Stacey because she rarely questioned me about my comings and goings.

When I awakened in the morning I felt that I hadn't used my best judgment. I was the lead detective assigned to the Corie Simms's case. I felt that I needed to remove myself from the case. I called my captain and set up a meeting with him so that I could turn over the information that I had already gathered on the case and to inform him that I knew the interested parties too well to be objective because I had every intention on continuing my relationship with Troi, no matter what.

As I lay in the bed with my arms around Troi, thinking about my life and how unhappy I was with my family situation at home, Troi interrupted my thoughts.

"What are you doing up so early?"

"I couldn't sleep. I guess I really need to be getting out of here."

"You alright?" she asked.

"Yeah, I'm cool. You alright?"

"Never felt better."

"Listen. I need to get going. I want to see you later on in the week. Is that okay?" I asked.

"I don't know if that's such a good idea. I know now is probably a terrible time to have second thoughts but I think we should have kept our hormones under control," she said.

"Oh, so you think that I was just getting my creep on? Is that what you think?" I asked.

"Well, come on, it definitely wasn't about love," she stated.

"C'mon, Troi. You know that I've always felt for you. I can't even believe that I'm here with you. I never even thought that I would be fortunate enough to share the same air with you. I enjoyed what we had last night, and I want to keep that going.

BEWARE OF DOG!

I like you a lot and I think you already know that," I responded.

"Yeah, well, the only problem is that I have a fiancé and your wife is married," she stated.

"We're both adults. I think it's safe to say that I'm not happy in my marriage and obviously you're not ready to get married. Now, that doesn't mean that I'm going anywhere at the present moment but I think we're both mature enough to find happiness in the midst of what we're both going through at home. You know it's not written anywhere that you have to be married and miserable," I said.

"I hear you. As long as we both know the rules. I don't know what I'm going to do about this wedding, but we're just keeping this easy right now."

"Now you're talking my talk. I know all about the rules. Who do you think invented them?" I asked.

"Oh, don't think you're going to be playing me with all the rest of those women you're probably out there fooling with. If you're seeing me then that's all you're seeing. Understood?"

"Troi, do you know that I don't even have sex with my wife? I mean, I'm not trying to put our business out there but just let it be known that you're all the woman that I need. I'm not seeing anyone but you, and you can count on that," I declared.

"As long as we have that understanding then we're good to go. Speaking of which, you're going to have to go. I gotta pick Corie up from the hospital. And make sure you let your captain know that you're no longer working this case. Something tells me that all hell is about to break loose," Troi stated.

"I'll call you later on," I said, quickly getting dressed, thinking of what I was going to tell Stacey. Then again, knowing Stacey, she probably wouldn't ask. That was her main

problem. She acted as if she didn't care what I did. It was as if I had a revolving get-out-of-jail-free card. If Stacey had put her foot down once in a while I probably wouldn't be the way that I was. I mean c'mon, it's not like she didn't know what I was out there doing. I guess for now, I had absolutely nothing to worry about. I had the ultimate in side honeys. Troi was a prize any day of the week. What man wouldn't want her? And then, I had everything under control at home, right?

"He who learns, teaches."
—African proverb

Chapter 11

Stacey

My day couldn't get any better. Xay has really gone and fucked up now. I know the asshole usually stays out all night, but that was it, I'd had enough. But, I had it all figured out how I was going to fuck him over in the long run. By the time Xavier got home, I was heading out the door. I was decked out in my blue, pinstriped pantsuit and I was in an exceptionally good mood. It's not every day that you get to settle on your dream house. After dropping the kids at day camp, I had made arrangements for my mother to keep them so that I could take care of my business.

"You look really nice today. You have a meeting or something?" Xavier asked as he entered the bedroom.

"Yeah, something like that. Where were you last night?"

"Didn't you get my note?" he asked.

"Yeah, I got it, but you were out all night," I said, just to mess with him because frankly, I could give a damn.

"You see, what had happened was," Xay began to lie. I could just tell.

Whenever Xay is about to lie, he always begins with,

well, what had happened was. It's something I've noticed over the years.

"Look, I've gotta run. I'm sure I'll hear from you later on," I said, walking up to him, giving him a long, wet kiss on the cheek.

He looked at me strangely, probably because I rarely even want to look at him, let alone kiss him, and then I just left the room. I gathered up the kids and headed out the door.

After dropping off the kids, I told them I'd be back to pick them up in a few days from my mother's house. I had so much business to handle.

I drove down to the Fraternal Order of Police Credit Union and parked my car in the lot across the street. Chris was waiting for me in the parking lot. It was imperative that she be there, since she was co-signing on my new house. Although Chris wasn't moving in, yet, she would be spending a lot of time there.

All of my life I've had to struggle just to get by. I can't say that I've ever met anyone that was financially secure, that is until I met Chris. The woman is brilliant. For starters, she's a self-made millionaire. Between the money her parents saved for her when she was born and her real estate investments, she's pretty well off.

I can't say that I know much about the stock market, but Chris has taught me so much in such a short time. Chris can work the stock market like she should be working on Wall Street or something. She taught me that I should invest in companies which make products that I just can't live without. Six months ago I began investing in companies which produce household products and I've seen a return already. Of course I'm not touching the money. The best type of investor is the one who allows the money to grow. Chris taught me that too.

BEWARE OF DOG!

Chris is truly unique. Born to a Vietnamese mother and a black father, she has the prettiest bronze complexion that I've ever seen. Her parents have been together since they met and married in 1962, during the Vietnam War. The one thing that Chris's mother instilled in her daughter was for her to save, save, save. Although I've seen her financial portfolio, and she's loaded, she has no qualms about sharing her wealth with me, but I'm going to make sure that I pay her back each and every penny that I've borrowed from her.

If someone would have told me that I would be in love with a woman, I know I would have smacked them silly. Hell, I'm not prejudice or anything, but I've never understood homosexuality—that is until Chris. If a person asked me how it is that a woman can be married to a man and only be attracted to men her entire life and then suddenly wakes up gay, I guess I would explain it like so: women have a general need for companionship first and foremost. We love to talk and love to have someone listen to our hopes, dreams and desires, and let's just face it, men are only in tune with the damn television. What better person to share all of that with than another woman?

Sometimes when people get married, it's more than for lust than love—at least that's the way it was for Xavier and me. In the beginning, the sex was off the hook with Xavier, but then I started needing more than just a roll in the hay. But, it was all very confusing for me. My feelings were emotionally out of control. I thought my feelings for him were love, but I guess, looking back now, it was just lust. Anyway, as time went on, the sexual, lustful feelings slacked off and so did the communication, and I would argue if we really ever had real discussions of merit. This is where I became vulnerable with Chris.

BEWARE OF DOG!

Our relationship began with friendship. Our time together started as companions, which led to trust, which ultimately led to intimacy. And so our story began. I became fascinated with her the whole time our friendship continued developing. I was intrigued by her and then one day, after one of our many long talks, I asked Chris out on a date. I couldn't even believe that I was asking her to be romantic with me. For goodness sake, I'd never even approached my husband for sex or had ever even given him a blow job, but I was enthralled by her. Anyway, Chris took me out to lunch and she just talked and talked my head off until I thought I was going to lose it. I wanted her in the craziest way. I'd never wanted anyone that badly. She took me back to her place, which is located on the Pier on Delaware Avenue. When I walked into her condo, I immediately felt safe and secure, and I knew that I was making the right decision.

That was ten months ago and now I know what true love feels like. I mean, don't get me wrong, I love my kids and in a strange way I even love Xavier, but Chris, makes me feel like a real woman. I would say that it's true, women are much more in tune with a woman's body than a man. I guess it's because we know what we like in regards to love, lust and romance and trust me, I'm satisfied. I am a firm believer that any woman if she meets the right woman at the right time can fall for another woman and give in to the curiosity of a woman-to-woman romance, right?

"It is not what you are called, but what you answer to."
—African proverb

Chapter 12

Corie

When I find the asshole who jacked me up, it's going to be some consequences and repercussions to pay. My head was hurting me so badly when I woke up. I used to get migraine headaches when I was a teenager and they hurt like hell, but if you're ever unfortunate enough to get a concussion, I promise you'll be praying for a migraine—concussions hurt that badly. Here I was all messed up in the hospital and goodness knows how Vanita was running my business.

Sunday morning, my parents and Troi came to the hospital to help me home. Troi had called me on Saturday evening and told me that she was staying at my place. Thankfully, she also warned me that someone had broken into my home and cracked open my safe. Now, there are only two people in this world who even remotely knew about my safe, and that was Troi and Malcolm. I knew that my girl was going through some problems with her man and that was the reason she was staying at my home but something told me my girl was about to be damn near a widow. Unfortunately, I had about

BEWARE OF DOG!

fifty-three thousand dollars in the safe. Now, before you go calling me dumb and what-not, I always keep that kind of cash on hand. You never know when you're going to have to bail somebody out or something. But, on the real, not to worry because my real money is tucked away safely in an off-shore account. My baby, Lance, taught me about that. If I had to guess, I'd say that I'm sitting on two million. I had a great year in the market last year and thankfully, I had my money invested in some Enron stock for more than three years and sold about two months before that whole fiasco went down. I know so many folks who got taken on that deal, but I made out like a bandit. That deal put me in financial security for the rest of my life. I tried getting Malcolm to get out, but he was one of the many people who lost his shirt in that mess. Anyway, Malcolm knew about my recent status with that money, and things were just beginning to fall into place that Malcolm wasn't the person who had my back like I thought that he did. But for now, forget that money that was in the safe. What was important to me was all of my financial documents that were inside. Those papers were worth more than that money. All of my banking information, I.D. numbers to my off-shore account and even my password was in there.

When I got home I tried like all hell to get my parents and Troi to leave. I had so much business to take care of but each of them kept doting on me, and of course they weren't about to leave me in that house alone. Finally, my parents agreed to leave, but only if Troi would stay with me. Unbeknownst to my parents, Troi had no intention of going back home any time soon.

"Troi, I need to ask you a question," I stated once my parents were out the door.

"Yeah, I think Malcolm has something to do with this,"

she stated before I could begin my interrogation.

"How did you know that was what I was going to say?"

"I know you. I also know that you're probably plotting your revenge if you think that Malcolm has crossed you," she said.

"Troi, you know that I love you like a sister, and we've been friends since we were born, but business is business. That's why I never wanted to have you get involved with Malcolm and my business ventures. I was afraid that something like this would come between us one day."

"Nothing like this will come between us. When Malcolm crossed you, he crossed me. I can't stay with a person who has deliberately lied to me, and just look at the way that he's been treating me lately. I don't know what's gotten into him, but it's painfully obvious that our relationship is over."

"But you know that blood is thicker than water and that sometimes a relationship between a man and a woman can supercede even the best friendships," I stated.

"You're my blood. The same way you kept me out of things in the past, continue to do so. What you have going on with Malcolm is between you both. In other words, handle your business," she stated.

"That's music to my ears. Now, if you don't mind, I've got to ask you to go shopping, go to the movies or do whatever the hell you want or need to do, but I've got to handle some business, so you need to leave me alone."

"Will do. I've got some errands to run, but I'm on my cell phone if you need me."

Once Troi was gone, I took the liberty of doing an inventory. As it turned out a few of my financial papers were missing, mostly tax records and some statement sheets but my password sheet was still there, and some other important

documents that I needed were all intact. Now, that's not to say that someone hadn't copied the information, but as it looked, whoever had busted open my safe, didn't know for what they were looking. It seemed they were more interested in the cash they stole and not the financial papers. Now that threw me for a loop. On second thought, maybe Malcolm wasn't the one who had broken into my safe because he would have known exactly what papers for which to look.

I returned all of the documents to the safe and then my cell phone rang. I looked at the Caller I.D. It was Lance.

"Hey, baby. What's up?"

"Where the hell have you been? I left you several messages," Lance stated.

"Long story."

"I've got time. I wanna see you this afternoon. Are you free?" he asked.

"Actually, baby. This is not a good time for me," I said, letting out a deep sigh.

"Talk to me. I hear tension all in your voice. What's up?" Lance asked.

"Where do I begin? Let's see. I was in New York, visiting with Troi and then I decided to come back early. Someone tried to burn down my club, and they cracked me over the head. Oh yeah, my cousin Lisa is still in the hospital in a damn coma," I responded.

"What! I'm on my way over," Lance stated.

"No, no. I look like shit. Don't come over," I pleaded.

"I'm not in love with your physical appearance. I love you. I'll see you in a few. Can I bring you anything?"

"Naw, just come on. I'm missing you," I stated.

I was actually glad that Lance had decided to stop by my house. Although I'm a big girl and I can take care of myself, I

BEWARE OF DOG!

just didn't want to be left alone, and Lance was always such good company.

I tried busying myself by straightening up my house as I waited for Lance. My home phone rang, and I damn near tripped over the rug as I tried racing for the phone.

"Hello."

"You're a dead bitch. Slut!" a low, raspy voice stated into the receiver.

"Who the fuck is this?" I asked.

"You're one dead bitch. You need to be taught a lesson."

"Well bring it on, motherfucker. You've got to bring yours to get mine," I stated boldly into the receiver.

"Die, bitch!" the voice stated again before disconnecting the line.

I'm not going to lie and tell you that call didn't bother me but I wasn't going out like some little nut from punk city. I just had to make sure that I kept my heat turned up. You know, make sure that my gun stayed loaded at all times, remain on top of my game and not let anyone catch me sleeping. I decided to take a quick shower before Lance arrived. As I climbed the steps to do just that, the doorbell rang. I peeked through the keyhole and there was Lance, my baby, looking all too good, on my doorstep.

I opened the door slowly and Lance came barreling in.

"What's going on? You okay? Damn, your eye looks red. Are you alright?" Lance asked.

"Ain't nothing. Yes, I'm fine, and my eye will be alright. I've just been rubbing it," I replied.

"Come on, tell me what I can do for you," Lance stated.

"You can come upstairs to take a shower with me," I stated, walking up to Lance, putting my arms around his waist.

126

BEWARE OF DOG!

"Come on, baby. Sit down and talk to me," Lance replied, taking my arms from around his waist and sitting me on the couch.

"Look, Lance. You know that I'm not the type to get all down in the dumps. I'm fine. Everything is going to be alright. Don't start worrying."

"Corie, why do you have to always be so damn hard? I'm not trying to take over. I just want you to know that I'm here for you."

"I know you are, baby, but I've got everything under control. Can you stay with me tonight?" I asked.

"When have I ever been unable to spend the night with you?" Lance asked.

"Good point."

Lance and I continued conversing about the incident, and I brought him up to speed on everything that happened— from Rashan's threat to how I ended up in the hospital. After he gave me the third degree like he was a damn detective, I convinced him to take a shower with me. I even tried to get in a little lovemaking, but Lance just wasn't having it. He was too worried that I hadn't fully recovered, but he was able to service me orally. Lance should have received a gold metal for his performance because each time he performed oral sex on me, I was definitely in for a real treat.

He slowly parted the lips of my vagina and began sucking and sucking on my clitoris until I damn near passed out. Lance can get a little freaky from time to time so when he stuck his fingers deep inside of me, I let out a loud sigh. He slowly glided each finger in and out until I could feel my juices running down my leg. Lance began to insert each of his fingers one by one, deep inside of me. He even threw in his thumb for good measure. He then began licking each of his fingers. I tried

BEWARE OF DOG!

to touch his large penis to bring him a little joy, but he held down my wrists, while whispering in my ear, "This is all about you. I want to make you feel good." Not one to argue, I laid back and took advantage of just relaxing. Lance then got up from the bed. "I'll be right back," he stated.

"Where the hell are you going?" I stated.

"I'll be right back. Here, take this hand and keep yourself busy while I'm gone. I'll be back in thirty seconds flat."

Lance ran downstairs while I kept the party going. He had placed my middle finger inside of my vagina, and although it wasn't his finger, I was bringing myself closer to an orgasm.

"Alright, thanks for keeping it moist for me. I got this now," he stated, placing a plate and a bottle on the nightstand.

"What do you have there?" I asked.

"Ssssh. Don't say another word. You can do all of the screaming, moaning and groaning you want, but don't say another word," he instructed.

I closed my eyes and waited anxiously for what was to come. Suddenly, I felt something cold inserted into my vagina. I then felt Lance's warm mouth suck whatever it was—probably grapes, feverishly—out of my walls. I damn near jumped off of the bed. I realized that Lance had reverted to his old ways. The first time he had inserted a strawberry in me, while he gently nibbled on the strawberry, I climaxed instantly, and this time was no different.

Lance then took a sip of wine and then kissed me on my mouth, slowly inserting the cold liquid. He then took another gulp of wine and slowly allowed the contents of the liquid to be disbursed over my body. I arched my back in delight, which put my nipple directly in Lance's mouth. He began sucking it like a hungry breast-fed baby. It was mixture of pain and bliss, but I

BEWARE
OF
DOG!

definitely didn't want it to stop.

Lance took yet another gulp of wine and then traveled to the area of my body that he loved pleasing all too well. He allowed the cold liquid to run slowly from his mouth, while I felt the chill of the wine inserted inside of me. He began sucking feverishly, like he was a dog who had lost his bone. Just as I thought I was going to enter into a coma from the pleasure, I had the biggest orgasm of my life.

"Come on. I need some in the worst way. Give me some baby. Please," I begged.

"Nope. I'm going to sleep," Lance stated.

"Baby, I know that I told you that you were always welcome here but you're going to have to go home now. There's no way that I can lay here all night with you and not jump your bones," I replied.

"Are you serious? I can't believe you're kicking me out," Lance stated.

"I'm not. The decision is all yours. Either you can give me some more pleasure or you're going to have to bounce. You've tortured me enough. Now what's it going to be?" I asked.

"I can't leave you here all alone. I'll wait until Troi gets here first. Where is she anyway?"

"I told her to hit the road. I needed some R&R. She should be back within another hour or so. Go ahead on home, I'll be fine.

"You sure?"

"Positive," I responded, putting on my favorite T-shirt and cotton shorts.

"I'll call you in the morning. You need to get some rest anyway. Call me later on if you need me, and I'll come right over. Get some rest, baby," he stated.

BEWARE OF DOG!

"I can't believe you're going to do me like that," I replied.

"One night of abstinence is not going to kill you. Give me twenty-four hours so that I can make sure that you're okay and I'll be back to give you everything that you want and desire," Lance responded, kissing me on the forehead, gathering his belongings.

When Lance left, I heard him punch in the alarm code, and I think before he was actually in his car, I was fast asleep. Although Lance had left me horny as hell, I was tired too. Sometimes I just don't know when to call it quits. I turned on the ceiling fan for the soft noise, got under my covers and was fast asleep. I was in a deep-like coma when I awakened to the worst sound a single female ever wants to hear, my home alarm blaring. I instantly fell out of the bed, disoriented. I quickly ran for my gun, which was nestled safely behind my headboard. Or at least that's where it was usually kept. But this time it wasn't there. Who the hell knew that I kept it there, or better yet, where the fuck was it now? No time for questions. I had to get the hell out of danger. I heard footsteps coming up the steps, so I had no choice but to run into the back room and lock the door. I pushed the bed up against the door. The handle was being jiggled, so I ran to the window and did the only logical thing, I jumped out. Luckily for me, I hadn't parked my Range Rover in the garage, so my fall was relatively easy. I searched my secret location under the bushes for my extra set of keys and thankfully, they were still there. I jumped into the Range and peeled out of there as fast as I could. Someone was definitely on my ass, and I had to get to the bottom of it before I was a thing of the past.

As I made my mad dash, I realized that I had no phone, purse, or anything. When I had gotten a good distance away, I

BEWARE
OF
DOG!

stopped at a twenty-four-hour convenience store and called
Detective DeVoe. He instructed me to remain at the store and
within minutes he was there.

"What happened?" Detective DeVoe asked.

"I was asleep and the alarm went off. I went to reach for
my gun, which I always keep behind my headboard, and it was
missing."

"Does anyone have the code to your alarm?" he asked.

"There are three people who have the code and that's my
boyfriend, Lance; Troi and Malcolm, Troi's fiancé," I explained.

"Well, it's safe to say that the person who tried to break
in either didn't know that you had an alarm or just didn't know
the code. You said your gun was missing. Who knows that you
keep a gun there?" he asked.

"I don't think anyone knows that. It's not something
that I publicize," I stated.

"Do you have somewhere to stay tonight?" the detective
stated.

"Yeah. I'll be fine."

"I'm going to send a patrol car over to your house.
Have a look around. Give me a call in the morning and we'll
get together and go back over to your house," he stated.

I decided to go to my parents' home. That was probably
the safest place for me. My mother tried to give me the third
degree, but I just told her that my ribs were hurting and I
needed some of that Guyanese loving care. That was enough
for her to lay low and stop asking me a million and one
questions.

The next morning I was eager to call Detective DeVoe
and get back home. We agreed to meet at my home at 10:00
AM. I arrived on time and Detective DeVoe was already there.
When we walked into my home, I hardly recognized the place.

BEWARE OF DOG!

It was trashed as if a damn rock 'n' roll concert had been held there. There were several things that were broken, such as lamps and priceless artwork. I was really pissed because I had met this artist, Robert Jefferson, from Yeadon and he had painted a beautiful print for me of a woman holding a baby, as she sat reading the Bible. Well, whoever the asshole was had placed a knife through the middle of the Bible. That was some sick shit. Thankfully, I still had Robert's business card so I could order a few extra prints from him once things settled down.

The scariest part of everything was the messages that were left on all of the mirrors. It read, YOU'RE GOING 2 DIE WHORE!

By now, you've all learned that I'm no punk bitch, but I need to keep things real. I was truly scared, and that ain't no bullshit. Someone wanted me dead, and for once in my life I had no control. I had to get things in order or else I was going to lose everything. I could regain control, right?

"Yesterday is today and today is yesterday."
—Natosha Gale Lewis, Author

Chapter 13

Troi

When it rains it pours. My life was literally in a shamble. Shit that I said that I'd never do well, just say, Mommy always said, "never say never." I'm in an I guess you could call it a relationship with a man who has made me feel like I've never felt before. I don't even know who the hell I am anymore and what I even represent. You know love, lust—call it what you want—will make you do some foolish things. I've seen Xavier every day for the past three weeks. Someone is out to kill my best friend and her life is falling apart as well. What the hell was going on?

Xavier was finding that he was just too heavily involved in this whole fiasco with Corie, and although we had discussed removing himself from the case, especially since my fiancé had turned out to be a major suspect, he never actually did.

Corie and I decided that we needed to get away from the stress of everyday life so we went on up to our family's timeshare in the Poconos. Besides that, someone was out to do bodily harm to Corie, and we had to play things safe. Corie was

BEWARE OF DOG!

visibly shaken, and that's so unlike her, but then, no one has ever threatened her before. Since someone had broken into her home, she had received threatening emails and phone calls at her house and her office. The last straw was when she had finally returned to her club, someone had left a bouquet of dead flowers outside of her office with a card that read, THIRTY DAYS UNTIL YOU MEET YOUR MAKER, BITCH!" Corie couldn't take it anymore, so we decided to head up to the timeshare, not telling anyone where we'd be, except our parents and Xavier. I was surprised that Corie hadn't told Lance, but she just told him she'd be in touch and would talk to him when she returned. I think at that point, Corie didn't trust anyone. Besides that, I hadn't seen or heard from Malcolm in two weeks.

I received a call from Malcolm telling me that he wanted me to meet him at Zanzibar Blue for lunch at 1:30 PM sharp. When I arrived at the restaurant five minutes late, Malcolm wasn't there. It was bad enough that I had fit him into my schedule at the last minute. I waited, calling him constantly on his cell phone. Each time I tried, I got his voicemail. By 2:00 PM, I was furious, so I ordered a grilled chicken Caesar salad and headed back to the office. When I got back, my secretary informed me that Malcolm had left three messages telling me that he would see me at home later that evening. I tried calling him again at his office, but I didn't get an answer, which I thought was strange. Again, I tried calling Malcolm on his cell phone but I didn't get an answer. I decided to leave early from work. I mean, it wasn't like I could concentrate anyway. When I arrived home, I found Malcolm upstairs packing two large suitcases.

"Where are you going?" I asked.

"Look, Troi, I'm sorry about this afternoon. I've got

134

some things I need to work out. I'm going away for a few weeks. I'll be in touch," Malcolm stated, brushing past me.

"What the hell do you mean, you're going away for a few weeks? You can't just leave and not tell me what's going on. What kind of shit are you caught up in?" I asked.

"This doesn't concern you. If anyone calls or comes looking for me, you don't know anything. This is for your own protection," Malcolm stated.

"Malcolm, you're scaring me. Please tell me what the hell is going on. I think you owe me that damn much," I stated.

"You're right. I'll tell you this. I owe some folks a lot of money. Remember that investment property down on Delaware Avenue that I told you about two years ago? Well, to make a long story short, I borrowed some money to come up with my share, and the investment fell through. You know those South Philly boys don't want to hear that shit, if you know what I mean," he explained.

"Don't tell me you've got caught up in some mafia crap," I stated.

"Naw, nothing like that. It's just a little more complicated than that. You'll be fine. No one is going to hurt you. I just need to get away for a few weeks and come up with a way to get the rest of this money. Relax. No one is going to get hurt. I'll be fine, baby."

"Fuck that. I'm not worried about your ass. I just don't want to wake up with a damn horse's head in my bed. I see you're so concerned about me. Hell, you weren't even going to tell me what was up. What would have happened if I hadn't come home early?" I asked.

"I was going to leave you a note."

"A note. Is that all I'm worth to you? Is that what it's come to?" I asked.

BEWARE OF DOG!

"You know we're better than that. I love you."

"You don't know the meaning of love."

"That's cold, Troi."

"Does this have anything to do with Corie?" I asked.

"Somewhat. It's complicated. I really can't get into this right now. I've got to go!" Malcolm stated.

"I just want to let you know that we're through. For you to walk out on me like this, not knowing what I have to face is cruel. I want you out now. You can take your keys if you want to because I'm going to have the locks changed."

"I'm sorry you feel this way but I don't have the time to get into this with you now. I'll be in touch within the next few weeks," Malcolm stated as he tried to step toward me and place a kiss on my forehead. The look on my face made him do an about-face.

After Malcolm left, I sat on the bed and cried for about two hours straight. I had never even contemplated the idea of being unfaithful and now, just three weeks after I had begun a "thing" with Xavier, my fiancé had left me, not for cheating, but for something that he was caught up in, but wasn't sharing what that something was. After I cried my contacts out, I called Xavier and told him what had happened. It was then that he admitted that he had decided to finally excuse himself from Corie's case because some of the evidence was pointing toward Malcolm, but he couldn't discuss that with me. It seemed that no one was telling me anything, and it was pissing me off!

The phone rang suddenly. I leaped for it and tripped on my huge wooden bed, causing tremendous pain on my big toe. I was certain that it was broken.

"Hello. Who is it?"

"Is Malcolm there?" a man's voice came blaring on the

BEWARE OF DOG!

line.

"Who is this?"

"This is Tremaine. Is this his fiancé?"

"Excuse me, do I know you?" I asked cautiously.

"You just ought to," he said sarcastically.

"What the hell is that supposed to mean?"

"Are you his fiancé or not. I think there are things you ought to know about your future husband. He's really caught up and someone should really pop your collar about what's going on with him," Tremaine stated.

"Look, I'm his fiancé. We're getting married in January. What the hell is going on? If you're one of his business partners, he's told me all about the whole situation," I lied.

"Partners, no, I have nothing to do with any of that," he stated

"What the fuck are you talking about then?" I asked.

"Look, Miss, I don't know how to tell you this, and maybe it's not my place to tell you, but, you really should get tested."

"I know you're not saying what I think you're saying," I said, my heart sinking to the bottom of my stomach.

"And exactly what are you saying?" he asked.

"Are you saying that Malcolm is seeing another woman?" I asked, hoping that wasn't the case, yet again.

"Sweetheart, a woman is the least of your worries. Your man is on the down low."

"What the hell is the down low?" I exploded.

"I guess you don't read much. It's been all over the newspapers recently. Every news station in the city is exposing the ugly truth."

"Listen, there must be some kind of mistake. Are you implying that Malcolm is gay?" I laughed.

BEWARE OF DOG!

"Yes, sweetheart. We all made a video and then I found out that my boyfriend, Steve, and Malcolm have been getting their freak nasty on, hot and heavy. I will tell you this. I do have HIV."

All I know is that I passed out, just after the phone fell on my big toe that I hit earlier. Between the pain in my foot and the pain in my heart, both knocked me out. Anyone would be ready to die after hearing something like that, right?

"Every exit is an entry somewhere else."
—Tom Stoppard

Chapter 14

Malcolm

      I'm in deep shit now and I don't know how I got caught up in this mess. To say the least, I've been exposed. How in hell did I get caught up like this? Here I am about to have my latest, best-selling group, Seven Down, release their sophomore project and now this. I'm being extorted by Steve, the guy I was kicking it with and his faggot-ass boyfriend, Tremaine. They've got me by the balls and don't want to let go. I received a call from Steve today and he told me that unless I give them two million dollars, they're going to expose me to the entire music industry. That fucking faggot Steve even tried to put me on blast on the Colby Colb Morning show on 103.9, The Beat. You see, Colby is practically a Philadelphia legend in the radio industry and he has this bit that he does called True Confessions. Steve called Colby and told him all about our situation and then he convinced Colby to replay a voicemail of me trying to get some ass from Steve and there I was, my voice, on the radio, unbeknownst to me, for all of Philly to hear. Thankfully, I was just waking up and my voice didn't sound like my own. Now, with that tape of the show and some other

BEWARE OF DOG!

footage Steve and Tremaine claim they have of Steve, myself and this other boy by the name of Rakweon, in a ménage a trios—they're blackmailing me.

To make matters worse, I received two phone calls from Troi and Corie, screaming bloody murder about them killing me.

"You faggot motherfucker!" Troi screamed into the phone.

"What? What the hell are you talking about?" I asked cautiously.

"Don't you play dumb with me. I can't believe you're a fucking queer."

"What are you talking about?" I refused to admit to anything unless she had proof.

"Your boyfriends called here and were kind enough to send me a tape outlining what they want from me, money! Oh yeah, now, I know all about your lifestyle. You down low prick!" she continued to scream.

"Troi, you need to calm down. We'll get the money, baby," I stated calmly.

"So that's what you were talking about earlier. There's no deal that fell through. These sissies are after you because you're a fucking faggot and they're trying to extort you and now you've got me caught up in this mess too," she screamed.

"Troi, you know a lot of people are always trying to bring a brotha down. You know there is nothing sissy about me. Now, let's put our resources together. I've got most of the money. Can you come up with five hundred thousand? And by the way, I ain't on no down low. That tape was technically altered."

"You think I'm stupid? That's why they call it the down low. There are no signs of detection to tell if someone is gay. I can't believe you exposed me to AIDS. I swear before God, let

BEWARE OF DOG!

me have a disease and see don't I kill you dead. Bitch-ass motherfucker!" Troi, screamed before hanging up the phone.

I felt terrible. She was right. How could I have been so careless? I sat there on the hotel bed and thought long and hard about what to do. The only solution would be to pay the money to these guys. But where would I get it? I know this is wrong, but over the years, I've been able to stash a few dollars here and there from Corie. I know, I know, it's wrong, but trust me, in the music industry it happens all of the time. That's why you have to always be the one to sign your own checks. Initially, Corie didn't do that and it cost her, big time, but she'll never miss it. Troi and I had a joint account for wedding expenses and I was able to cash in that account already. Of course she wouldn't be thinking I got to that money so soon. But, it was only for one hundred thousand dollars. Between my investments, the money that I accumulated from Troi and Corie and the money from my record label, I could come up with 1.5 million, immediately. Getting my hands on more money this fast was going to take some time. As greedy as Steve and Tremaine were, they'd probably be satisfied with that. But, then there was the videotape that they could always use to extort me for more money. These guys had evidence that I was a down low, fudge packer—on tape. If that tape got out, my career as a notorious record executive was over. Then again, I could always have Steve and Tremaine erased from the face of the earth for much less. I mean, really, who would miss them, right?

"Smooth seas don't make skillful sailors."
—African proverb

Chapter 15

Troi

The next morning, I ran to my doctor's office and demanded that they test me for everything—from HIV to clahmydia. If I had it, I wanted to know about it. Corie is the complete opposite of me. We've had this talk several times about STDs and HIV and she told me that she never wants to know her status. Her running joke is, "I'll be limping around at two pounds and in denial that I have anything." I don't think that's funny. If I have a disease, I want to know about it so I can get adequate treatment. Early detection can save your life. Look at Magic.

I explained to Dr. Mack that I had to have my test results immediately and he sent me right over to the lab. I guess he could see the severity of the situation and told me that he'd call me back before the close of business with my results.

All day long I was on pins and needles. Corie had called me to see if I wanted to go to the Poconos with her and I didn't think it was such a bad idea. After all, if I did get results that said that I was HIV positive or something, a mountain was a good place to hurl myself from. Although I was scared shitless, for some reason, I wasn't going totally crazy. If my results came back positive, which I hoped they didn't, I was going to do everything in my power to educate women about safe sex. But, damn, I surely hoped that my results were negative.

It's peculiar that when speaking of anything negative, that's usually something bad, but when it comes to STDs, positive is not something that's good.

I was sitting at home and my phone rang. I checked the Caller I.D. and noticed it was Corie.

"Hey," I said, trying to sound upbeat.

"You ready? You're still going with me, right?" Corie asked.

"Yeah, I'm still going. I'm just waiting on an urgent phone call.

"What's up?" she asked.

"Nothing much," I lied.

"You know you can't lie to me. You sound stressed. What's wrong?"

Before I knew it, I broke down crying.

"What's wrong?" she asked, just then, my other line clicked and I said hold on. I looked at the Call Waiting Caller I.D. and noticed it was Dr. Mack's office.

"I'm coming over. I'll be there in five minutes," Corie said.

Before I could protest, she hung up the phone. I didn't really want to see her if my results were positive.

"Dr. Mack?"

"Yes, Troi. I know you're anxious to get your results and everything came back negative. You have a clean bill of health. Now, that's not to say that you don't still need to get tested, regularly," Dr. Mack stated.

BEWARE OF DOG!

"I know, doc. Thank you so much. You've really made my day. No, make that my life," I said, the weight of the world being released from my shoulders.

"Now, Troi, do you need some condoms? You really shouldn't be having unprotected sex. Even if it is with your fiancé," Dr. Mack warned.

"I don't Dr. Mack. I use the birth control patch, but we still use condoms as a back-up, but there have been occasions where we didn't use condoms. But, you can best believe that's not happening ever again," I vowed.

"Alright, Troi, if you need anything, just give my office a call. Have a great weekend," Dr. Mack said.

Just as I was hanging up the phone, Corie knocked.

"Come on in," I stated with a tear-stained face.

"What's up, sis? Talk to me," Corie said.

"Girl, you're not going to believe the night and morning I had. I don't even want to tell you. You have no idea how embarrassed I am," I said.

"We're closer than sisters. You can tell me anything and not have to worry about shame. It's not even that kind of party with us. Talk to me," Corie said.

"I received a package in the mail today. Have you had lunch yet?" I asked.

"No, why?" she asked.

I got up and popped the tape in the VCR. There were three men, whom by now, I had pieced together were Steve and Tremaine, but just as clear as a sunny day, there was Malcolm. Who couldn't see him? He was knee-deep in shit, literally. While he was screwing Steve, Tremaine was underneath Steve, sucking on his penis. It was the nastiest crap I'd ever seen.

"Turn it off. I think I'm going to be sick. What the fuck was that?" Corie stated.

BEWARE OF DOG!

"That was a tape of my fiancé and your business partner. Apparently, these two guys, who have no image that they care about, are extorting Malcolm and me. They want two million dollars, or they're going to the press."

"Fuck them! You don't owe them shit! This ain't your fight. Your main concern is to get tested for HIV and other STDs, and fast," Corie said.

"I did. First thing this morning, I called Dr. Mack. He was nice enough to give me my results. I have a clean bill of health. Thank God. But, now I need to come of with that money. Can you imagine the type of negative press I'll get? I wouldn't even be able to pay a client to represent them."

"You don't have that kind of money," Corie stated.

"I spoke to Malcolm, earlier. He says that he needs about five hundred thousand more. I can take out a loan against my business, but I have employees now. I can't do that,"

"I can't take this stress. Are you packed and ready to go?" Corie asked.

"Yeah, let's go. This is more than I can deal with right now," I agreed.

On the way to the Poconos, Corie and I had a real heart to heart.

"I need to tell you something," I began.

"Now what? I told you I can't take the stress. Don't lay nothing to heavy on me," Corie warned.

"I know that I'm always on you about seeing married men and now I've gone and royally screwed up now," I said.

"What is it? Just spit it out. You know I'm not the one to judge folks, especially you."

"I've been seeing Xavier. Thankfully, we used condoms. I'm really feeling him. Now, especially with all that's come out about Malcolm, I don't know where this will leave us," I stated,

BEWARE
OF
DOG!

ashamed of myself.

"Look, you're grown. Just be careful. He is married and it's not like he's going to leave his wife for you. You're the one who's basically single now. Plus, you've got a lot of shit to clear up before you start something new," Corie said.

"Yeah, but when Xavier and I first became involved, none of this other shit was going on. You're right though, I do need to make a clean break from all that's going on right now between Malcolm and me, first," I said.

By the time we arrived at Mount. Pocono, the sun was setting. The cabin Corie's family owns was moderately decorated. Corie, who of course was still paranoid since she had her own problems, was strapped with a double-barrel shotgun, and she kept her 10mm on her at all times. Even in the shower she'd take that damn shotgun. Girlfriend was tripping, but I couldn't blame her. She even made me strap up at night when I went to bed. One of the main reasons that I had decided to go with Corie, besides the obvious of being with my best friend, was the simple fact that I was scared staying at home by myself, not knowing how desperate this Tremaine and Steve would get if they didn't get the money they wanted soon. As far as I knew, someone could be coming up in there trying to do bodily harm to me, right?

BEWARE OF DOG!

"I'm just a gay man in a woman's body."
—Natosha Gale Lewis, Author

Chapter 16

Troi

According to the calendar, it was day twenty-nine. Corie went into action. She slept most of the day away and set her clock for 11:00 P.M. By midnight, Corie was ready for whatever was to come. She took a long, hot bath and listened to an Al Green CD. Once she came out of her bedroom, I hardly recognized her. Corie had her long hair pulled tightly back in a bun. Although she rarely wore makeup, she applied this green Army type of concoction on her face. Dressed in all black, she donned a scarf, turtleneck and a pair of black Royal Robbins equipped with side pockets. In short, she looked like a damn Ninja. Corie was ready for action. She had an eighteen-inch machete, Mace, rope and of course she was strapped with at least three guns—one on the ankle, one in on her side pocket and one in her holster.

"What are you auditioning for a lead role in a Lord of the Rings movie?" I asked.

"Now is not the time for jokes. I gotta do what I gotta do. If someone comes in here to take mine, then they're going down too. I ain't going out like no damn punk," Corie

responded.

I had never seen the look of death in Corie's eyes. She meant business, and I had no doubt that somehow, we'd be alright.

The clock struck midnight, and it was officially day thirty. Corie and I were both on edge. I tried to pick up my cell phone to check my messages, but couldn't get a signal. I reached for Corie's, and she damn near had a heart attack.

"Don't use my cell phone!" she yelled.

"What's up your ass?" I asked.

"My bad. It's just that I don't know if someone can trace that damn thing. I'm not taking any chances. I only brought it in case we had to call for a body bag on somebody. Otherwise, I haven't used that thing since we left."

"Okay, that was smart. You're really thinking on your feet."

Several hours passed, and nothing was going on. I began to get a little sleepy, just sitting there. I had brought up three books that I hadn't had the time to read. I had Azarel's, A Life to Remember, T. Wendy Williams', Confessions from the Jumpseat and Natosha Gale Lewis's Only Fools Gamble Twice. I couldn't figure out which one to read first because I had heard they were all great books. Since I had met Natosha Gale Lewis before at a book signing at Empirian Books, I decided to read her novel first. Plus, she was a down to earth sista from Philly.

As I had expected, the book had me on edge. One of the characters, Delaney Love was the type of guy that I wished Malcolm could be. As the plot intensified, my heart was pounding as Corie was wearing a damn hole in the carpet.

"Oh shit! Get prepared! A car just pulled off the main road and is heading this way," Corie said, turning out all of the lights.

BEWARE OF DOG!

She peered through her night-vision goggles as she crouched down on the floor. I ain't gon' lie, I was scared stiff. I'm not all tough like Corie. I'm the cute one. Corie used to always be down for a damn fight. Me, I was too busy applying my lipstick and playing with Barbie while Corie was playing with the guys who wanted to "play" with Barbie. It was do-or-die time. I had to strap up and step up to the plate. I kept reminding myself to think like Corie and I'd be alright.

"I'll be right back. If I go down, you make sure you blast whoever tries to come up in here, because you can best believe they ain't trying to leave no damn witnesses."

"Where the hell are you going? Don't leave me up in here. I'm going with you," I said, getting up off the floor.

"Stay down. You want to get your damn head blasted off? Stay right there. I'll be back. We don't have time to debate this shit," Corie said as she lay on her stomach and crawled out the back door. I heard the car come to a stop. Whoever the culprit was was bold as hell to just pull up to the front yard. Next thing I know, I hear a sound like a person in a bad Kung Fu movie. It was Corie. Hyah! Then I heard a thump.

Corie came running back in. "It's Xavier. I knocked him out cold. Come help me get him in the house." I ran outside and we dragged Xavier in. It was quite a feat, since he's six-four and estimating his size, was about 220 pounds.

"Go get some cold water, so we can throw it on his face," Corie stated.

I ran to the kitchen and got a glass of cold water. When I came back I almost dropped it.

"What the hell are you doing?" I asked.

"What does it look like? I'm gonna hog-tie his ass," Corie stated.

BEWARE OF DOG!

"Get the hell off him. He ain't the bad guy."

"How the fuck do I know that? I ain't trusting nobody right now."

"Girl, stop tripping and untie him," I stated, moving in to untie Xavier before he woke up and arrested both of our asses.

"Alright, but I've got my heat on his ass just for safe measure. If his ass so much as flinches, I'm gon' be Big Bertha's bitch in jail, 'cause I'm gon' smoke his ass."

"You've been watching that damn movie Menace II Society again, haven't you?" I asked as I untied the rope from Xavier's legs. I poured the water on Xavier's face and he instantly woke up.

"What the fuck?" he asked, rubbing his head where there was huge lump where Corie had hit him with the butt of her gun.

"Sorry, baby. You okay?" I asked.

"Damn. Who hit me?" he asked.

"Yours truly. Nice to see you," Corie stated dryly.

"Why the hell did you do that?"

"Uh, news flash. Someone wants me dead and no one knows we're here, so when I see headlights coming toward my house and this just happens to be day thirty, you can understand why I'd be a little on edge. Got that, detective?" Corie stated.

"Hold on. I'm not the bad guy here."

"Well, I don't know that. I've got to protect my ass. What brings you here anyway?" Corie asked.

"Damn. Good to see you too. Anyway, baby. Sit down," Xavier instructed, turning toward me.

"What's wrong?" I asked.

"I tried calling your cell phone but your voicemail kept coming on. I left you three messages," he began.

BEWARE OF DOG!

"Just spit it out. What's wrong?" Corie asked.

"Malcolm has been shot. He's in surgery right now," Xavier stated.

"What!" Corie said.

"Is he going to make it?" I asked.

"I don't know," he responded.

"Omigod. I've got to get to the hospital," I stated. "Come on, Corie. We've got to get packed."

"Naw, you go. Malcolm is the last person I want to see right now," she stated.

"You're not going? You can't stay here by yourself."

"I know. I'm going to drive to the airport. I think I'm going to go home for a few weeks."

"Home? Home where?" I asked, not truly thinking.

"Guyana. That's probably the safest place for me right now. I need to clear my head and get back on top of my game. You go. See about Malcolm. We need to know what's really going on," Corie stated.

"Fuck him. I'm totally through with his ass. That could have been me that's laying up in that damn hospital. You think he cares enough about me to make sure that I wasn't caught up in all of this dumb shit?" I stated angrily.

"Whoever shot Malcolm definitely didn't want him dead unless they just don't know how to shoot. In my professional opinion, they're just sending him a warning. I think there's more to it than what we see," Xavier stated.

"Oh, yeah, you're right. That's the last thing they want is to see him dead," I said.

"Why do you say that?" Xavier asked.

"In my personal opinion, I think they just want money, but they're trying to let Malcolm know they mean business. Malcolm is greedy and I know that Malcolm is out to just save

151

BEWARE OF DOG!

his own ass," I said.

"You want to make a statement?" Xavier asked.

"What's being said is between the three of us. You're not even on the case anymore," Corie stated.

"True that. I don't know nothing. As far as I'm concerned, Malcolm is putting my baby's life on the line, and he's lucky I don't bust his ass for that shit," Xavier said, pulling me on his lap.

"Alright, if y'all going to start that mushy shit. I've got to go pack."

"What about me? Where am I going to stay?" I asked no one in particular.

"You're welcome to go with me if you want. I'm sure your aunt Lynette would love to see you in Guyana," Corie stated.

"Yeah, I can go for some of her macaroni and cheese and roti too," I thought, imagining being home with my family.

"You can stay at my place," Xavier offered.

"Huh? I don't think your wife would like that too much,"

I stated.

"Oh no. My aunt has an apartment that I rented from her a while back. It's completely furnished and everything. All I have to do is make a call."

"That would be a good idea since no one knows about it," Corie suggested.

"Alright. If it's not too much of an inconvenience," I stated.

"For you, anything," Xavier stated, planting a wet kiss on my lips.

"I think I'm going to be sick," Corie responded, placing her hand over her mouth. "I do need a favor from you, Troi. I

BEWARE OF DOG!

just need you to tie up some loose ends for me at the club since you're going to be staying here."

"Whatever you need, whatever you want, you've got it from me," I stated.

Corie made her airline reservations using my laptop and it cost her a small island to go home, but she was unconcerned about the amount. After I packed my bags, Xavier and I used the remaining time to get a little closer.

"Thanks for letting me stay at your aunt's house. It's not going to be a problem, right?" I asked.

"Baby, if I could give you the world, I would. Do you remember when you gave me that stick of gum me last week?"

"Yeah, but what has that got to do with anything?" I asked.

"I'm still chewing it," Xavier confessed.

"What? What's the deal with that?" I asked.

"It's the closest I could get to you. Troi, I know that we've only been kicking it for a few weeks, but I'm feeling you. I'm not gon' lie, I haven't been the most faithful man in the world. But with you, it's different. I can't stop thinking about you," he stated.

"I know. I feel the same way about you. I know I should be thinking about getting out of the situation I'm in right now with Malcolm, but you're a welcome change."

"Come on, let's get the hell out of here so we can get you straight," Xavier said.

"Oh, that's funny," I said, thinking of my current situation.

"What's funny?" he asked.

"You said you wanted to get me straight. Now is not the time to tell you everything that's really going on. I've found out some things about Malcolm that I don't even want to talk

BEWARE OF DOG!

about right now, but we'll discuss it later," I said.

"Come on, love, let's bounce," Xavier said before kissing me on the forehead. I knew that we were playing a dangerous game of Russian roulette, but we were both adults and could handle whatever came our way, right?

BEWARE OF DOG!

Part II

The Showdown—

It's About to Go Down.

"Send a man where he wants to go and you see his best pace."
—African proverb

Chapter 17

Corie

How the fuck did the person who was after me find me? I'll tell you. It was that damn cell phone. It'll do it every time. Y'all don't believe me, do you?

It happened when my dumb ass just had to have a little piece before I left for my trip to Guyana. I made the reservations for my trip, but the only time that I could get a flight out was on a Tuesday morning. It was Sunday afternoon by the time Xavier, Troi and I got back to the city. We dropped Troi off at the hospital so she could check on Malcolm. Xavier went with me to my house and apparently the attacker must have been camping out, just waiting for a sista to show the hell up. My place was ransacked, yet again. I'll tell you this, whoever it was sending me all of these messages was definitely going to be receiving a cleaning bill from me because I didn't appreciate how they kept tearing up my shit. I mean I had my lamps especially made in South America and my furniture doesn't come cheap.

Anyway, I packed my shit for about three weeks and I

BEWARE
OF
DOG!

took my important financial papers out of the safe, because quiet as it's kept, South America is where my long money is stashed. So, that's where I needed to be anyway.

I called Lance from my cell phone and of course, he went into damn near cardiac arrest because he hadn't heard from me. Like the great business investor that he was, he took over the operations at the club so that everything ran as if I were there. Of course my employees were freaking out, but once they received their paychecks, they pretty much forgot all about me. Lance had been staying at the club night and day, thinking quickly on his feet, trying to make the same decisions that I'd make. I was so glad that he was in my life. It was then that I felt truly horrible for not telling him that I was even leaving town. It was something that a person who was in love with another person would do. So, I had to question my own feelings for Lance. I knew that I loved him, but I just couldn't allow myself to get all googly eyed with a man that was married. Hell, that was the primary reason why I only dealt with married men. They were emotionally unavailable and Lord knows I had issues in the emotional baggage department. But, Lance stepping up to the plate in a time of need really let me see that this was more than just a fling. We had a bond that couldn't be broken.

"Where the hell have you been? You didn't call me and I was worried," Lance asked, concern dripping from his voice.

"Baby, I told you someone is out to put a sista on permanent lock. I had to get out of dodge for a minute," I stated.

"I know that, but you couldn't leave me a note, a phone call, email, something?" he asked.

"Baby, I haven't been thinking straight. I was a little on the paranoid side," I stated.

BEWARE OF DOG!

"You're not saying what I think you're saying, are you?"

"Hell no. I trust you more than I trust myself. I know that I can count on you one hundred percent," I stated honestly.

"Where are you? I'm coming to get you," Lance stated. "I do need to see you before I leave again. I'm horny as hell," I stated.

"Hold on. Now where are you going?" Lance asked.

"I'm going to Guyana. I need to take care of some business and stay out of dodge. The shit is hitting the fan left and right. Have you heard about Malcolm?" I asked.

"How could I not have? It's been all over the news. You know how it is when someone gets shot downtown. The media acts as if it's a World War III going down. Don't try to change the subject. Why are you leaving again?" Lance asked.

"I just told you."

"See, when you say that shit, it makes me think you don't think I can take care of you. Before you start mouthing off, I know that you don't need someone taking care of you, but I've got your back. Stay with me and let a man—me—take care of you for once in your life."

"I can't stay at my house and what about your wife?" I stated.

"Corie, I left Sherrie last week, while you were away," Lance stated quietly.

"What! What happened?" I stated in utter shock.

"I just got tired of living a lie. We've never loved each other, hell we don't even like each other. I've told you time and time that it was for societal purposes. Sherrie started talking about getting pregnant, and I decided it was time to get out before things got too complicated. I even went to see my lawyer already. Of course my parents are threatening to disown me if I go through with this, and Sherrie's father and my dad

158

BEWARE
OF
DOG!

have been over to my place about a hundred times this week to talk me out of embarrassing the families' name. But I'm my own man. I've made enough bad mistakes to continue down the path that I'm on. Whatever happens, happens, as long as I can eat and be with you, that's all that I need. Are you down with a broke brotha?" Lance asked.

"Lance, fuck that money. This whole ordeal that I've been going through has taught me that money ain't shit if you don't have a life to live. You'll be alright."

"I know I'll be alright, but will we be alright?" Lance asked.

"What are you asking? If I'll be your girl or something?"

"I'm asking if you've got my back and will you allow me to have yours? Let's be there for each other. Only us. Not that tired-ass dude who keeps coming in here looking for you trying to play hard and what-not. I had to step to my man the other night. He kept mouthing off so I had to show him how a real man gets down. I don't think we'll be having any problems out of him anymore," Lance stated.

"Oh, that was Rashan. Screw him," I stated.

"I'd rather not. Anyway, are you down with it being just you and me?"

"I'm down with you," I stated.

"I've been staying at the Ritz Carlton. Meet me at the club after you've finished packing. You're staying with me, indefinitely."

"Damn, you sure know how to take charge, don't you?" I asked, loving the fact that for once in my life I wasn't in charge and someone, a man, was leading. I was willing to follow Lance.

"Let's get this straight. We're equals. There are going

BEWARE OF DOG!

to be times when I'll lead and you'll follow and vice versa, but in this particular case, I'm wearing the pants. Now, bring your ass. I'm missing you like crazy. Meet me here and we'll go home together," Lance stated.

"Whew! I like to hear that. I could get used to hearing you refer to your place as home," I said.

"This is only the beginning. I've got plans for us," Lance stated.

"Do you now? Do tell," I said.

"I'll show you better than I can tell you. Just know that I love you," Lance stated.

"Damn," was the only word I could muster in my mind. I knew that what Lance and I had was deep, but I didn't know that he felt that strongly about me. I certainly was beginning to feel those love-like feelings.

"See you soon, baby. Don't keep me waiting too long."

"I'll be there within the hour," I stated.

I hung up the phone all excited and what-not. It had been so long since I was in a committed relationship, and I didn't want to mess things up. I was going to be the best damn woman to Lance that I possibly could. I knew that things weren't quite normal for him at home, but I wanted to show him what it was like to really be feeling a woman.

Xavier was snooping around my living room the entire time I was on the phone.

"Now I think I'm going to be sick," he said, faking as if he was going to throw up.

"Why are you all up in my business?" I asked.

"Just hurry up and get packed. I've got things to do."

"You can go. I'll be alright," I stated, hoping he wouldn't leave.

"Please. I wouldn't dare leave you. Troi would have

160

my ass on a platter," he stated.

I finished gathering my belongings and was soon ready to hit the road. I was excited about staying with Lance, but I still needed to go to Guyana and get that money out of those accounts before Malcolm and his crew found out about the loot I was sitting on. I had kind of figured out what was going on but I still had a few pieces of the puzzle to put together. If I used the left side of my brain to the best of my ability, I could only figure out how Malcolm had come up with the type of money he had already forked over to the gay dudes. Plus, I had my theory on who was harassing me. It was probably John Frabizio, the most ruthless man in the underworld. He had been pressuring Malcolm to get me to sell the club, due to its prime location, and I had no interest in selling. I never in a million years figured John Frabizio would resort to these senseless acts, but then again, it wouldn't be the first time I was wrong, and it damn sure wouldn't be the last. When I arrived at the club, Lance had it locked down like it was Fort Knox. I tried convincing Xavier to let me off at the front door, but he wasn't having it. He insisted on walking me to the front door and literally handing me over to Lance. I think he wanted to make sure he got a good look at Lance too.

When we walked in, we expected to find Lance in the bar, but he was nowhere to be found. I guess Xavier's cop instinct kicked in because he told me to wait by the front door as he crouched down and withdrew his gun from his holster.

"You strapped?" he asked. I looked at him as if he were stupid or something, because you know Miss Thang always has the heat on. "You have your cell phone?" Xavier whispered.

"Yeah," I responded.

"Dial 911. Tell him there's an officer who needs assistance."

BEWARE OF DOG!

I did as I was told. I was scared shitless. Suddenly, all of the lights went out in the already dark club. I knew that the shit was about to hit the fan, for real. I then heard a gunshot then footsteps running upstairs. I pulled out my gun and maintained my position. I guess it was the man or the cop in him, because Xavier took off running toward the stairs. He was gone for about five minutes, but it seemed like an eternity. I heard two sets of footsteps coming down the stairs, just as the other police officers came running through the door. Just then I heard the familiar sounds of my future baby daddy's voice. It was Lance, and Xavier was right behind him. I was never so glad to hear Lance than I was at that moment.

"What the hell happened?" I asked, running over to Lance, hugging him tightly.

"I'm okay, baby. Are you alright?" Lance asked.

"I'm fine. Will one of you tell me what the hell happened. Please!" I demanded.

"Just calm down, shortie. He's about to tell you now," Xavier stated.

"I don't know. I was down here cleaning up and getting ready to close up shop as I waited for you. I saw you two pull up so I ran upstairs to get my coat and lock up the office and I saw someone running out of the office at the end of the hallway and when I yelled out to them, they shot at me. Thankfully, they missed as they climbed out the fire escape," Lance stated.

"Did you get a good look at him?" I asked.

"Naw, the lights went out, and I couldn't see a damn thing," Lance stated.

"Shit. We're no closer to finding out who this asshole is. Now do you see why I want to go to Guyana so badly? Come on. Let's close this club up and be out. This can all be replaced," I stated.

BEWARE OF DOG!

"She has a point, man. Why don't you two go on and lay low for a minute," Xavier said.

"Alright. This shit is getting out of hand," Lance agreed.

"I got my ticket. Let's just go. We can stop by the hotel, get you a bag and your visa and be out. I don't even wanna pass go. I just want the hell out of this city for a minute," I stated.

"Come on, let's bounce. I guess we're off to South America. I've always wanted to see my baby's roots anyway," Lance stated.

We arrived at the Ritz, and I began to feel a little calmer. Lance quickly packed his bag and we were off to the airport. We were going to fly up to New York and get a plane out of LaGuardia. You can catch a plane to any place in the world in New York. For now, I just wanted to feel safe, and it had been a long time since that happened. I knew that I would be safe with Lance in Guyana, right?

"The end of an ox is beef, and the end of a lie is grief."
—African proverb

Chapter 18

Xavier

If someone would have told me that it was going to go down like this, I never would have believed them. To put it mildly, Stacey ain't shit!

I was so busy helping Corie and Lance get on their feet, my own world was collapsing around me. True to my word, I called my auntie and hooked Troi up with my former apartment up on Germantown Avenue. My aunt Shirley was in the process of renovating the entire building and fortunately for Troi and me, she had just finished that unit, so it was ready for my baby.

When we arrived back in the city, I dropped Troi off at the hospital so she could visit with her P.A.M. (punk-ass man) and let that fool know that she was out. I escorted Corie over to her place to pack and then over to her club to meet with her man, but then all hell broke loose.

Corie and I entered the club and shit started getting strange. I didn't even have time to call for backup. I heard gunshots and what-not so I had to dive into action. I hated not knowing what I was walking into. I didn't even have on my

BEWARE OF DOG!

bullet-resistant vest because contrary to what people will have you believe, there ain't no such thing as a bullet-proof vest. All I had was my 40-caliber glock, but luckily, Corie had a heater on her, and from what Troi told me she was a great markswoman. I had her call communications and advise them that I needed assistance, and in no time that I heard the echoes of sirens blaring, confirming that several police cruisers were on their way. I was about to go upstairs, when I heard gunshots and then footsteps running down the hallway.

Once I got upstairs, I noticed a window was open and Lance was upstairs in the hallway. Since I had never met him, I pulled my weapon all up in his face, telling him, "Police, get down on the ground now!" Since he complied so easily, I didn't have to shoot his ass. I handcuffed him and patted his waist for weapons. Once I heard my backup coming through the doorway downstairs, I continued my search, checking the opened window at the other end of the hallway. All was clear, at that point I observed someone, but I couldn't make out the description of the person on the vacant building running to the far side, suddenly disappearing out of view. The shit was really weird and everything was happening so fast, and I was almost tempted to ask my captain to put me back on the case. I mean, yes, I had become personally involved with Troi, but that's exactly why I wanted to get involved, after all, I was feeling Troi something fierce. I know this sounds corny, right about now. I don't know if it's love or not, but I just know that Troi makes me want to be a better man. I wasn't feeling Stacey and I was tempted to just come right out and tell her that I was miserable and unhappy with her. Hell, I was tired of living a lie, and I just wanted to be happy. Troi did just that for me. I was smiling and shit, and although I knew that she and I both had issues to work out, I just wanted to do whatever it took to

BEWARE OF DOG!

make and keep her happy for as long as she would allow.

Anyway, after the fiasco at the club, I escorted Corie and Lance to the hotel, making sure that they were safely inside. I checked my voicemail and noticed that I had just received a message from my baby, Troi. I hung up the phone and called her instantly.

"Hey, baby. I just got your message. What's going on?" I asked.

"Nothing. I'm just leaving the hospital."

"How was it seeing Malcolm?" I asked.

"He's in guarded condition, but he still managed to cuss me out for not being there for him," she stated sadly.

"You gon' be alright?" I asked.

"As long as I know that I've got you in my life, things don't seem so bad after all," she replied.

"Where are you now?" I asked.

"Waiting in the lobby. I still need to go home and pack some of my things," she said.

"I'm on my way. I'll be there in a few minutes."

"Naw, I'm cool. I can just hail a taxi," she stated.

"I'm on my way. As long as you're with me, you don't have to catch a taxi. Again, I'm on my way," I said.

"I'll be waiting outside on Broad Street," she said.

I arrived at the hospital in record time since I was so close by. Troi looked absolutely beautiful, and she made me happy the moment that I saw her. I dropped her off at her house, telling her that I had to run a few errands. I figured, knowing women, she'd be about two hours packing everything that women pack. I shot up Germantown Avenue to the apartment. I knew that Troi was really going through it with her fiancé and having to leave her home, so I wanted the transition to be as smooth as possible.

BEWARE OF DOG!

I hit the Cheltenham Mall. I went inside of Liguorius Bookstore and got Troi a few books that I thought she'd like. I hit a few other stores in the mall, making sure I bought scented candles, satin sheets and some late-night snacks for my baby.

When I arrived at the apartment, I set everything up nicely. I lit the candles so that I could get that new-paint smell out of the rooms, I made the bed, putting baby powder under the fitted sheet and I made sure the place was clean as whistle. Everything had to be in order for my baby.

Troi called me and told me she was ready. I gave her the directions and she was on her way. I lit the candles and then took a shower. It had been so long since I had been with Troi since she was up in the Poconos, and I had been missing her like crazy. One night, after I had gotten off work, I was driving home and I thought of Troi and me making love on my motorcycle. I could just see her legs in the air, sitting on my bike, motor running and the vibrations of the bike bringing her further joy as I licked her like a sweet piece of candy. By the time I had gotten home, my dick was so hard, I was beginning to get a headache. I went into the bathroom and began jerking off, but even that wasn't working. I came out of the room dressed in my pajama bottoms and noticed Stacey laying on her side. She was fast asleep. I thought, for one moment of trying to relieve some tension by approaching her, but the second I contemplated that idea, my dick deflated. So much for that theory. That's when I knew that Stacey just didn't do it for me anymore.

After I got out of the shower, I began placing large amounts of shea butter—bay rum scent—lotion on my body. Ain't nothing worse than a bad-smelling man. I wanted to present myself in the very best for Troi. She did that for me. As I placed the last of the lotion on my body, the doorbell rang

BEWARE OF DOG!

and I knew it was my baby. I ran to the door in my towel, because you know a brother was looking good as hell. My pecks were on point. I opened the door and standing there was Stacey.

"Don't even try to deny it, motherfucker! I caught your ass red handed. Where's your bitch?" Stacey asked, pushing her way past me.

"Stacey? What the hell are you doing here?" I asked in utter shock.

"Don't look all stupid in the face. I should be asking you that very same question. You see, you think you're slick but just let me tell you this. A woman knows. What you do in the dark always comes to light, motherfucker!" Stacey said, waving her index finger all in my face.

"I ain't gon' be too many more of those motherfuckers. You can cut the bullshit right now. I don't know who it is that you think you're talking to but I ain't the one, two or the three," I said, checking Stacey while I stalled for time to think how I was going to get my ass out of this sling.

"Fuck you, Xavier. You ain't running the show anymore. I am. Now, you see, your Aunt Shirley called and left a message saying your apartment had gotten fumigated this morning so you might want to bring some fresh candles. I bet you didn't expect her to leave that damn message, now did you?" she asked.

Actually, I could have screamed. I told my damn aunt not to call the house, but I guess she had forgot my cell phone number and decided to call me at home. Fuck it. The cat was out of the bag. It was do-or-die time. Now was the time to let Stacey know that I was done.

"So, where's your bitch? I'd like to meet her. Who knows, I may be able to show her a thing or two," Stacey said,

BEWARE OF DOG!

going in the back, looking for the mystery woman.

I guess you can add up what happened next. You guessed it. The door was opened, so Troi walked on in.

"Honey, I'm home," she said, dropping her bag to the floor and running over to me, hugging and kissing on me. Before I had a chance to warn her what was going on. Stacey came running out of the room.

"Oh, so this is your new woman, huh? Oh, she's pretty. Hi, I'm Xavier's wife. Nice to meet you, bitch!" Stacey said sarcastically.

"Aw shit," Troi responded, I guess at a loss for words.

"Yeah, aw shit is right. Somebody better do some motherfucking explaining or else some shit is going to get busted up in here today!" Stacey replied.

"I think I better leave," Troi stated.

"Naw, you ain't gotta go nowhere. Stacey, don't be coming up in here threatening nobody. You ain't gon' do shit, but go the hell home. I'll see you later."

"Oh, you think you just gon' kick me the fuck out. You better tell your bitch to get the fuck out?" she demanded.

Troi tried to leave but I stopped her.

"Let her go. Get the fuck out, bitch! Fucking home wrecker!" she yelled.

As I reached for Troi's arm, she pulled free and then Stacey jumped over me and tried to punch Troi in the back of head, giving the ultimate sucker punch.

"Fuck that!" Troi yelled, turning around, ready for all-out war.

"Bring it on, slut. I've got something for you and him," Stacey yelled, going in her waistband and pulling out her gun.

I didn't have time to do anything but tackle her as my towel fell to the floor. Troi ran for cover. Before I could get to

her, a shot went off and penetrated the ceiling.

"Get the fuck off me, asshole. I'm going to kill you and your hoe. I'm sick of your fucking cheating ass. You gon' learn once and for all not to be sticking your dick in any and everything that moves," Stacey yelled.

Suddenly, the police rolled in and began yelling and screaming. "Drop your weapon, motherfucker!"

I thought they were speaking to Stacey rather harshly, but then when the officer moved in closer and hit my ass upside the head with his billy club, I figured out that I was still holding the gun as I felt my head hit the floor and the blood rushed down the right side of my face.

"He tried to kill me," Stacey yelled. "I'm a police officer."

Before I had a chance to utter a word. The two white officers swarmed on me like they were flies on shit. They began kicking and beating my ass until no tomorrow.

"Stop, stop. She's lying. He's a cop too!" I heard Troi yell.

I never stood a chance. The cops kept kicking my ass as I tried to shield my head from the blows. I don't remember much after that.

I awakened in Temple University Hospital. I was jacked the hell up. I had two broken ribs, a dislocated shoulder blade, a missing tooth and a headache from hell. I tried opening my eyes, but I only had one good one that I could open with ease. My left eye was glued shut and swollen beyond belief.

"Hi, baby."

"What the fuck are you doing here! Get the fuck out!" I stated through clenched teeth.

"I'm your wife. This is where I belong," Stacey stated.

"You're dead to me. I want a divorce the minute I can

170

BEWARE OF DOG!

walk or crawl out of this place. You ain't shit, and you're never going to be shit. I know that I've done some foul things to you over the years but this was totally senseless and uncalled for," I stated.

"I didn't mean to do it. You had me trippin'," Stacey said.

"You didn't mean to do it? Stacey, it ain't nothing to rap about. Just get the fuck out!" I yelled.

"No, I'm still your wife. What the fuck do you want with that bitch anyway?"

"She ain't a bitch and, besides, it's not about her anyway. This is about you and me. I'm the one laying up in some damn hospital all broke the hell up."

"Xavier, you know that I love you, baby. I've been good to you over the last twelve years and this is how it's going to end? Haven't I stood by you all of those times you fucked me over six ways from Sunday?" she asked.

"I never did any foul shit like that to you though."

"So, it's like that, huh? It's over? You're just going to walk out on me like that?" she asked.

"Stacey, you know damn well that we haven't been happy together for a long time, if ever. The only reason why we're together is for the kids."

The next thing I know, in walked two detectives from Internal Affairs. "Detective, we'd like to talk to you about the domestic violence charge that's pending against you," the shorter of the two detectives stated.

"What's it going to be?" You know I hold the key to your future in my hands," she stated, bending down closely to my ear.

"I stand by what I've said to you," I responded.

"Detective, I'd like to press charges formally against my

BEWARE OF DOG!

husband. I can no longer take his violent episodes," Stacey replied.

"What the fuck!" I couldn't believe my ears. After all the years that I had been married to Stacey, I never thought she'd sell me down the river like that. Not only could I be facing jail, but I would be automatically removed from the ranks of detective. They'd placed my ass on administrative duty, taking my service weapon, while totally humiliating me. This was all Stacey's doing. I knew I was in deep shit when one of the female captains walked in. I had no idea why she was there. I had never met her, although I had seen her fine ass on the news several times. Even though she was cute, I could tell she was a lesbian.

"Detectives, we'd like a little privacy," she stated. "I think you know who I am, Xavier. May I call you that?" she asked.

"Yeah, knock yourself out," I replied.

"Chris, what are you doing here?" Stacey asked.

"Someone want to fill me in on what's going on? How do you know her by her first name?" I asked.

"You haven't told him yet? You had me believe that he knew who I was," the captain asked.

"Oh, I think this is where it gets good," I replied, trying to sit up."

"Stay out of this, Chris. I told you I'd handle it," Stacey replied through clenched teeth.

"Listen, Xavier. I thought you knew. Listen up. Stacey and I have been seeing each other for close to a year now. We're all adults here, and this situation has been blown way out of the water. We can all stop this from getting further exaggerated. Did you tell him that you're even moving out yet?" Chris asked calmly.

BEWARE OF DOG!

"You mean to tell me that you put me through all of this shit for nothing? Trying to come up in the apartment like fucking Wonder Woman when you knew all along that you were cheating on me? Trying to make me look like the one who's a fucking snake?" I asked.

"Calm down, man," Chris stated.

"First of all, you're the cheater. I'm just experimenting," Stacey responded.

"What!" both Chris and I yelled.

"You ain't nothing but a fucking carpet munching diesel dyke," I yelled.

"Settle down, man. Stacey, can you excuse us for a minute. Xavier, let's talk man to man," Chris said.

"Fuck that shit. Fuck you and her, and technically I have the goods to do just that. Contrary to your beliefs you ain't no man. You're a woman. You see how I'm all broke the hell up. I'm suing the fucking PD. This shit ain't going down like that. As far as this hoe is concerned, you can have her stank dyke ass, but the kids are coming with me. I'll be damn if you think you're taking my kids from me and exposing them to this crazy gay bullshit," I stated.

"Let's go. See, this is why I needed for you to stay out of this shit. I told you I had this," Stacey responded.

They got up to leave. Before Stacey walked out she turned to look my way. "I'm sorry it had to end this way."

I took one look at her and spit on the floor. I was totally through with her. I just knew that my blood pressure was rising. As I tried to calm down, the only person I longed to see was Troi. At least I still had her in my life, right?

BEWARE OF DOG!

"Quarrels end, but words once spoken never die."
—African proverb

Chapter 20

Troi

If someone could explain to me why drama was
suddenly following me all over the place, that would be
fantastic. When I realized that Xavier's wife was in the
apartment, ranting and raving, I should have turned and just
walked away, leaving all of that nonsense between a husband
and his wife. I had no one to blame for all of this turmoil in my
life because I had caused it by getting emotionally involved
with a married man in the first place.

When Xavier was in there getting the shit beat out of
him, I ran over to the phone and dialed 911. I no sooner got the
last number dialed when Stacey ran over and snatched the
phone out of my hand. Blame it on the stress, but I smacked the
living daylights out of that broad. For a hot second, she looked
like she wanted to swell up on me. We stared eye to eye for
about ten seconds, and then she retreated to where the officers
were and yelled, "Stop, officer down!"

I know that Xavier and I were dead wrong. There ain't
no right way to justify what we had going on, but Stacey knew
damn well that Xavier hadn't laid a finger on her, and here she

BEWARE OF DOG!

was having the cops lay into his ass.

As quickly as the assault had begun, it was over. Both of the officers were panting heavily, trying to scramble on their feet as they contemplated their next move.

"Call for an ambulance. My client is in need of medical attention," I stated.

"Client? Ma'am?" the taller of the two officers asked.

"Yes, I'm Troi Stokes. I practice family law. You two are done. I'll personally see to that!" I stated.

I noticed the fearful looks on the officers' faces, and I immediately went into action. "Get some towels for the bleeding." I barked orders at Stacey and the two officers.

I knew how cops operated. To be honest, the entire situation was out of hand way too fast. The two officers, seeing a black man with a gun standing directly in front of a woman who later identified herself as a police officer well, you get the picture. Xavier didn't stand a chance in hell when the officers got the free ticket to lay into his ass. However, it didn't justify their actions, and I was going to see to it that Xavier got the best representation possible so he could formally bring charges against the two officers and we were going to see about getting Stacey brought up too. All if Xavier wanted to, of course.

When the ambulance came, I jumped in the back with Xavier. Again, Stacey tried to flex up in my face, but I had to check her.

"Where the hell do you think you're going? I'm his wife, unless you've forgotten,"

"Back off, bitch. If you're so much the loving wife, then you would have thought twice before you had the living crap beat out of him."

"This ain't over. I've got something for your ass too," Stacey replied.

175

BEWARE OF DOG!

"Promises, promises. Bring the noise anytime you want to get knocked the hell down," I stated, slamming the ambulance doors in Stacey's face.

It was kind of ironic that Xavier and Malcolm were in the same hospital. So once I found out from the intake nurses that Xavier was going to be okay, beside the fact that he was suffering from a major case of "brokendownness," I mean, my sweetie was looking quite bad, all bandaged up, I decided to go and check on Malcolm.

When I arrived at his room, I felt a cold chill run up my spine when I noticed that the person laying in his bed was an old Asian lady. Of course, I stepped back out of the room and looked at the number. Just what I thought, I had the right room. I saw Nurse Hudson, and ran over to her.

"Nurse, where's my fiancé?" I asked.

"Oh, good question. He left the hospital early this morning after the doctor made his rounds. I went back in to check on him two hours later and he was gone. He's not supposed to be out of the hospital. He was shot for heaven's sake," Nurse Hudson stated, looking at me as if had helped him escape.

"No one saw him?" I asked.

"Honey, I'm in the middle of a double. I saw two black guys coming in here last night during visiting hours and they went to his room. The only reason why I even remembered them is because they were fine, but they looked like they were bad business. You know the type of guys that you don't want to be messing around with or get caught in the alley with at night," Nurse Hudson stated. "After the two men left, I went in the room to take Mr. Cooke's blood pressure, and he looked like he'd seen a ghost. I asked him if he was alright, but he snapped my head off. Your fiancé needs some anger management

176

classes."

"What did he say?" I asked.

"He told me to mind my own damn business."

"I apologize for his behavior. He hasn't been himself lately," I replied, totally embarrassed.

"Don't sweat the small stuff. I've been a nurse for eleven years. I've seen it all. You've got to have thick skin dealing with people.

I excused myself from Nurse Hudson. I called Malcolm's cell phone, and he answered on the first ring.

"Malcolm, where the hell are you? I'm up here at the hospital and they told me you checked out. Will you tell me what the hell is going on?" I asked.

"Where's Corie? I need to talk to her. I've been calling her since last night and she's not answering her phone," Malcolm stated, completely ignoring my questions.

"Oh no, you don't. I asked you a question."

"Don't start, Troi. I need to talk to Corie. Now tell me where the hell is she?" he demanded.

"Who the fuck?"

"Troi, I don't have time to argue with you right now. Either you're going to tell me where the fuck I can find Corie or I promise both of you will pay dearly for ever even knowing me," he replied coldly.

"Fuck you, asshole. You're so fucking intelligent, find her your damn self."

"Troi, wait! I'm sorry."

"I know you are."

"I guess I deserve that. I'm just so stressed the hell out."

"Where are you, Malcolm? If you know something about what's going on with Corie, tell me. I'd better not find out you're the one who's coming at her," I warned.

BEWARE OF DOG!

"I have information for her. This may all be my fault," he said.

"Malcolm, is this about that damn tape?" I asked.

"No, it has nothing to do with that, but I was hoping that if I told Corie what I know, then she'd be grateful and loan us the other five hundred thousand to pay off these two guys. You think you can talk her into it?" Malcolm asked.

"Are you trying to bribe my best friend? After all she's done for you?"

"I don't have time for all of this. I'm trying to save both of our lives. These guys mean business. How long do you think it'll be before they send one of us a warning."

"Tell me what you want with Corie and I'll get the message to her," I said.

"I can't. The less you know the better it is for all of us. Now, where can I find Corie?"

"Why? Just tell me that much."

"Alright, Corie has a lot of money that she's sitting on. I made the mistake of running into someone and told him things about her that I probably shouldn't have. Now, I think this person is the one who's out for her," Malcolm stated.

"I think you're lying. I think you want Corie's money. You'll do anything to not let your precious little secret come out," I said.

"I'm trying to help you too. Once we're married, between your law practice and my record label, we'll be two powerful individuals," Malcolm said.

"Do you honestly think I'd marry someone like you? Malcolm, face it, you're gay," I said.

"I am not gay. Don't even say no bullshit like that to me. How could you say that? You know I love women."

"Do you even hear yourself? Didn't I see the

BEWARE
OF
DOG!

videotape?" I asked.

"I told you already. I just like a little different flavor every now and then. That doesn't make me gay. It says that I might be a freak, but never gay," Malcolm said.

"You're in denial."

"Now that I've told you all of that, how can I get a hold of Corie? I think she'll be pretty happy to find out what I know. Listen, I really need this money," Malcolm said.

"You have assets. Why can't you take out a loan or something?"

"You don't want me to go there right now," Malcolm said.

"What do you mean?" I asked.

"I've tapped into every available source already. I'm busted. I promise I'll pay you and Corie back every red cent."

"Malcolm, let's just go to the police and tell them we're being extorted. Don't you think these assholes will always try to bleed us dry?" I said.

"Yeah, that's why I have another plan. Listen, I've gotta go. I'll be in touch," Malcolm said.

"To hell with you, Malcolm. I don't care if you live or die. You hung my ass out to dry and you expect me to still be in your corner. We're though. Stick with what you know, and that's dick, seeing how you are one and everything. But, I think you've figured that out already," I said.

"I promise you. When this is over, I'm gonna make you pay for what you just said to me. Trust me, I'm going to find Corie, and when I do, you can best believe that I'll get that money, if it's the last thing that I do."

"Trust me, you and I both know that when you mess with Corie and her money, it will be the last thing that you do."

"Whew. I'm really scared," he said, hanging up the

179

BEWARE
OF
DOG!

phone in my ear.

I called Corie and got her voicemail. I knew that she was probably in the air, flying to Guyana so I was hoping that she would be checking her messages, once she landed.

I went upstairs to check on Xavier and he was in a deep sleep from all of the drugs the doctors had him on. I gave the nurse my cell phone number and asked her to call me when he woke up. I had to get to the bank, ASAP.

I hailed a taxi since I had left my truck at Xavier's apartment. When I arrived at the bank, I was seen instantly by a customer service representative. The $100,000 we had was originally in my name only, but since I thought I was sharing my world with Malcolm, we began a joint savings account for wedding expenses. I didn't expect that money to be there since Malcolm had alluded to the fact that he had tapped into all available assets. I did, however, have another account that Malcolm knew about that my parents had been saving for me since before I was born, putting the money in mutual funds. It took more thirty years, but the money had survived through the tough times of the investment highs and lows, and I was now sitting on a comfortable nest egg. Malcolm had always tried to get me to put his name on that account, but I'm no fool. Although I didn't have to change accounts, I didn't know what kinds of tricks Malcolm had up his sleeve that could get my money, but I wasn't taking any chances. After I had taken care of getting the money transferred to another account, I thanked the banking representative and made my way out of the door. As I left out of the door, my head was down, and who do I bump into, of all people? Malcolm. He had this crazed look in his eye, and I hardly recognized him. Before I could utter a word, I saw two big, black men, who I recognized from the tape as Tremaine and Steve, walk up behind him, and they looked like

BEWARE OF DOG!

they meant business. I was scared stiff. I didn't know what was going to go down.

"Pardon me, miss," Malcolm stated, pretending not to know me as he pushed past me.

"Keep it moving, Cooke," one of the men said, moving closely to Malcolm's back. If I didn't know any better, I'd swear it was a gun.

The way Malcolm had been treating me earlier and all of the mean and nasty things he said, left me feeling unsure about everything. I didn't have a person I could turn to for advice. I walked to the curb, waiting for a taxi. I looked through the window and saw the man who had just assisted me with my transaction, pointing at me. I then looked at Malcolm and he began waving his hand for me to leave. The two brutes came barreling out of the door and I ran into the middle of the street. A taxi stopped in front of me and I jumped in. "Uptown. Get me the hell out of here," I yelled.

I saw Malcolm run around the corner and he disappeared from my view. The brutes began chasing the car and that's when I noticed one of them had pulled out a gun. I ducked for cover and one of the bullets hit the back windshield.

"What the hell you got me involved with, lady?" the cabdriver yelled in his thick accent.

"Just step on it. Now!" I yelled.

The driver did just that and was able to get us out of the brutes' firing range. Once we were relatively safe, I told the driver to take me up to Germantown. I had to get my truck. Suddenly, Guyana didn't sound so bad. Not only was Malcolm's and Corie's lives in jeopardy, but now so was mine. I mean, now these thugs knew where I lived and could identify me. My life just wasn't safe anymore, right?

"Brother man...you got some spare change?"
"Get your ass a spare job, then you'll have some spare change!"
—Robin Harris, Comedian

Chapter 21

Corie

It had been three weeks, and Lance and I had been chilling in Guyana. It was so good to be back home. I mean, don't get me wrong, I was born in the States, but South America is where I'll always feel at home. The people, the land, the great-tasting food, it just all felt like heaven.

Lance and I stayed with Aunt Lynette. For all of those folks who know her, they know she's off the hook. She kept us well fed and definitely full of drinks with her infamous Bourbon Slush. I drank so many, I couldn't stop laughing at Aunt Lynette playfully flirting with Lance the entire time we were there. The night before we left, Auntie threw us a big bash, and all of my cousins and their friends stopped by the house to see us off. I had so much fun that I contemplated buying a condo so I could visit more often.

Before we headed to the airport, Lance and I stopped by the bank so I could transfer my money to an off shore account,

BEWARE OF DOG!

which I did without any complications. Having done that, Lance and I boarded the plane and were officially headed back to the States. When we arrived back in Philly, I knew it was going to be some drama, but I had no idea what was coming my way. I was tired of running and decided that I was ready to deal with whatever. I was tired of the dumb shit.

Lance and I were staying at the Ritz and his suite was beautiful. Lance had rented the penthouse apartment and I'm sure it was costing him a small fortune, but it wasn't like he didn't have the money. Surprisingly, once we unpacked, we realized that we weren't tired at all. I wanted to go to Bluezette, a popular downtown bar and restaurant where the young, urban professionals hang out, near Penn's Landing. They have the best apple martinis, and I knew that one had my name written on it. I was starving and I wanted to get out and get something to eat too. Looking back on things, I wish we would have stayed inside all night long. After all, it was going to be a long time before Lance and I would ever be close again, if ever the way we were before that night.

Just as we approached Market Street, my cell phone rang. I looked down and it was Troi.

"What up, li'l boy?" I asked, climbing out of the car.

"Where are you? When did you get back? Why didn't you call me before you left Guyana? Did you get my message?" Troi rambled on, not even allowing me to answer any of her questions.

"We just got back this afternoon. I'm doing well. Lance and I are down here at Bluezette's for a few drinks. Why don't you join us?" I said.

"Naw, I'm just going to stay in and work on a few cases. I'm so behind on deadlines. Girl, did you get my last message?"

BEWARE OF DOG!

"Yeah, I did. That's a trip about what happened with Xavier and his wife. I told you to be careful," I said.

"What are you doing tomorrow? Let's meet for lunch or something. We have so much catching up to do," Troi said.

"Deal. Come to the Ritz around one o'clock. Pick me up and we'll go someplace nice to eat. Your treat," I teased.

"Alright, call me if you need me," Troi said, hanging up.

Lance pulled his car up to valet. The door to Bluezette was only a stone's throw away, but a homeless man came from out of nowhere. "Brotherman, brotherman, can you spare a few dollars so I can get me something to eat?" Lance pulled out a ten-dollar bill and gave it to the man. I kept on walking to the door, pausing briefly to look at the young man. He looked vaguely familiar, but I kept on walking and stepped in the restaurant when the concierge opened the door for me.

Lance finally made it in and began telling me that the homeless man outside was telling him how he was down and out because he had lost his family and he was so depressed that he felt that he couldn't go on.

I wasn't trying to be rude, but I was hungry and I had problems of my own. I really didn't want to hear about this dude's problems. I mean, get over it. In life, you have obstacles and you either sink or swim, do or die. We've all had issues that could have caused us to fall down and not get back up, but some of us don't use our problems as a crutch. We just do what we've got to do.

"Baby, let's see if we can get seated upstairs," I said, cutting off Lance's story. I just didn't want to get depressed by hearing someone's sob story.

"Alright. Let's ask for Delilah," Lance stated, steering me to the hostess' desk.

It was crowded, I mean wall-to-wall folks. Thankfully,

BEWARE OF DOG!

Lance and I both knew the proprietor, Delilah Winder, so getting a seat wasn't a problem. We were seated within a few minutes, and I ordered the shrimp Caesar salad and Lance had the chicken and waffles. Of course we got our apple martini on and I was feeling good. The drinks were putting it on me. All I wanted to do was take Lance back to the hotel and do him properly, the way he and I both deserved.

We must have stayed at Bluezette for about three hours, just talking and laughing, and Lance then confided in me that he had called Sherrie while we were in Guyana and told her that he was prepared to do whatever it took to get their divorce. Lance told me that in Pennsylvania you had to be separated from your spouse for six months before a divorce was granted, but he was willing to do whatever it took to not have to wait so long.

"I'm not saying that I want to rush out of one marriage and into another one, but what I am saying is that I want you in my life, permanently. I'm too old to be out here sport fucking," Lance stated.

"What the hell is sport fucking?" I asked.

"Listen, you're a single woman and I'm a married man. Up until now, I could never ask you to not see another man because look at my situation. But, what I mean by sport fucking is that I don't want to be out here screwing this woman and that one like it's a damn sport. I love you and I want to be with you. Can you handle that? I mean, I know how independent you can be, so let me know if we're not on the same page."

"We are on the same page. I know I can be a little hard core at times, but I think that I'm ready to give this love thang a try again. But, I'll warn you, I'm scared of what the whole love triangle can bring sometimes, which is the risk of being hurt," I said.

BEWARE OF DOG!

"Love doesn't come in pretty packages, Corie."

"I know, but that's not what you see in the damn movies. Why can't it be that way? I've been through so much, I deserve a life without a little drama for a change."

"I can't promise you that we won't have some issues to deal with, but I can promise to love you the way you want to be."

"Come on, let's bounce. I'm getting tired, and all I want is for you to wrap your arms around me tonight and we'll deal with the rest of the drama tomorrow."

I asked Lance to drive by the club, just so that I could see what was going on. When we drove up to the entrance, the line was around the corner. From the looks of things, I'd say that Vanita had everything under control and suddenly, I didn't feel a need to be in control for a chance.

If Lance and I had been paying attention, we would have noticed the black Suburban with tinted windows following a half block behind us, but then, I was so wrapped up in everything that Lance was saying and my own personal thoughts that I wasn't on top of my game. I was thinking Lance and I would be able to overcome whatever obstacles came our way. No, we didn't have a match made in heaven, but only good things were coming our way. We had dealt with so much already. What else could go wrong, right?

BEWARE
OF
DOG!

"If you run after two hares you will catch neither."
—African proverb

Chapter 22

Xavier

Just when I thought that I had everything in life that I wanted and needed, the shit really hit the fan. I know this is going to sound crazy, and hell, it might sound a little fictional, you know the kind of shit you read in a book, but trust me, it's real. As a matter of fact, it couldn't get any more real than what I was facing.

Troi and I were getting along great. Troi is a neat freak and so am I, so practically living together was no big deal. Of course, nothing good lasts forever. Troi was pretty much hanging out at my apartment with me every day. She really wasn't going in to her office on a constant basis until we knew the whole deal with Malcolm and all of the drama that was going on with him. After all, some strange things were going on. Stacey was even laying low. I should have known that she was up to no good, but then again, in my wildest dreams, I never would have suspected some crap like this to go down. I know you're wondering what the hell I'm talking about, so I'll explain it the best way that I know how.

A few years ago, I was involved in a car accident while I

BEWARE OF DOG!

was on patrol. It was during the time that Stacey and I were trying to have a baby, before Ayanna was born. Stacey was having a really hard time getting pregnant at first. Since she was approaching thirty, she was freaking out because she just couldn't seem to get pregnant. At first we didn't worry too much because at least we had one child and we knew that both of us could have children. But then, after two years of trying to get pregnant and nothing, Stacey allowed her stupid-ass girlfriends to talk her into seeing a fertility specialist. At that point, I thought it was crazy to waste good money because I just figured that Stacey was worrying too much and that was probably the reason why she wasn't becoming pregnant in the first place. Finally, the doctors ruled out anything wrong with Stacey and you know what they wanted to do next? You guessed it. They wanted to start testing, probing and prodding on me. I mean I did my part initially by getting the series of tests, but I thought that was it. Of course every man in the world is against that. But women, especially women of color, can be feisty as hell and most of the time, they get what they want. So, Stacey was on me left and right to get checked out even further. I finally gave in. I went to the specialist reluctantly and after the first visit, they concluded that my sperm count was now even lower than the first time they conducted the tests, due to the car accident. In a nutshell (no pun intended), the doctors wanted to store my sperm, just in case Stacey and I had any problems in the future. I was cool with that because at least I didn't have to go under the knife. You know that I wasn't having that. I went through the necessary procedures to get my little homies frozen and stored and then after all of that worrying and carrying on, Stacey pops up pregnant anyway. So I guess my little men were good to go from the start.

BEWARE OF DOG!

Well, you'll share my surprise when I get a damn bill in the mail from my insurance carrier one week ago. I'm getting this bill from a fertility specialist, after all of these years. The bill had the nerve to be for thirteen hundred dollars. A brother man is doing alright, but now with the divorce looming and all of this bullshit back up in my face again and the fact that Stacey would definitely be trying to file for child support, it was no telling how much I was going to have to shell out this time. Of course thirteen hundred dollars wasn't going to come easy.

I figured there must be a mistake so I contacted the billing department and they referred me to the doctor's office to handle it directly. After telling my story to about three different people, finally, the fertility doctor himself spoke to me.

"Mr. DeVoe, how are you doing?"

"I'll be better when you tell me why I'm getting a bill from your office for thirteen hundred dollars," I stated.

"Certainly. As you know, when you and Mrs. DeVoe came to my office, I explained to you, that although you paid your storage fees to the lab that houses your sperm, when you were ready for retrieval and the insemination process, you would be charged accordingly," Doctor Westbrooks stated.

"That's fine, but we didn't have the sperm retrieved, nor did Stacey have the insemination process conducted."

"Ah, sure she did. I just did the procedure two weeks ago. I just gave Mrs. DeVoe a call and told her the good news. Fortunately, the process worked this time, which is miraculous that it worked the first time. Congratulations, Mr. DeVoe, you're going to be a father."

I'm nobody's punk, but you know I was about to pass out. "I see," I stated, the only words coming to my mind before I lost consciousness.

"If there's nothing else. I have a patient waiting to see

BEWARE OF DOG!

me. It was great speaking with you and give my regards to your wife," Doctor Westbrooks stated. I knew damn well that the only regards I would be giving to Stacey were my condolences before I killed that bitch.

So, there it was. I had finally found a woman whom I could learn to love and she was everything that I ever wanted, but what woman would stick around after that bullshit? I know my black Nubian sistas are strong, but how much more could I put Troi through and expect her to be in my corner? On the other hand, Stacey knew that her ass had that procedure done and never bothered to let me know. I just didn't know what I was going to do next. It didn't take me long to decide, because the shit came to me. The doorbell rang and as I peered through the peephole, there was Stacey.

"Open the door. I know you're in there."

"Fuck," I muttered under my breath.

"Fuck you too. I heard that. Now open the door."

I snatched the door open, giving thanks that Troi wasn't there.

"I just came by to tell you that I filed for divorce today and child support too."

"What the fuck did I ever do to you to deserve this shit that you're giving me?"

"For starters, you couldn't keep your dick in your pants since I first met you. You thought I was a stupid-ass woman who was going to take your shit for as long as you wanted to give it to me? Fuck that. It ain't nothing stupid about me. I'm sharp with mine. Whenever you think you're two steps ahead of me, think again, because I'm hip to you. Now you're just getting back everything you've done to me. All those nights that I cried over you. Huh, I don't feel no pity for you. Now, Chris could show you a thing or two about how to treat a lady."

190

BEWARE OF DOG!

"So, when are you going to tell me that you're pregnant by having the insemination done? If you think I'm going to let you and your dyke bitch raise my kid, you've got another thing coming. Don't think I don't know why you all of a sudden popped up and got pregnant. Because despite your she-man treating you like she's a real man, she'll never have what it takes to be one," I said, grabbing my dick for special emphasis.

"What?"

"Yeah, you heard me. You're so fucking smart, but I changed my address, and as long as the insurance is in my name, the bills still come to me. Now, answer my question."

"That is none of your business. Stay out of this."

"What the hell do you mean? Of course this is my business. You're trying to get me caught up in some old dumb shit. If you think you're taking me to court for child support on this kid, you're sadly mistaken. Don't think for one minute you and your she-man are going to play Barbie and Ken on my dime, while using my children as a damn guinea pigs."

"Don't worry, I'm not going to ask you for a damn thing. Like I said, stay out of this. I'm warning you."

"Who the hell do you think that you're talking to like that? As long as you're trying to carry around my seed, that is my business."

"Look, I didn't come here for all of this shit. I just came to tell you about the separation."

"And you couldn't call me on my cell phone to tell me that?"

"Why do you have to talk to me like that? What did I ever do to you? All I ever wanted was to love my husband and build up on our family, but you just walked all over me. But I'm not upset with you. I'm more upset with me for allowing it," Stacey said. "You don't have anything to say?"

BEWARE OF DOG!

"There's nothing left to say."

"Just like that? We've been married for twelve years and you're just going to let it all go down the drain without so much as an explanation?" Stacey asked.

"Stacey, let me ask you this question: If I'm such a piece of shit, than why are we even having this conversation now?"

"I never said you were a piece of shit. I will admit that you have some issues that you need to deal with regarding fidelity."

"Then why would you want to stay married to a man who doesn't make you happy?"

"Xay, don't get all caught up in yourself. You screwed my life up. I'm going to make sure that if I can't have you, won't nobody else want your broke ass. I'm gon' get pregnant as many times as I can. If I can't break your spirit, than I'll break your pockets."

"The difference between you and me is that I realize that I have issues, but what kind of shit are you on? If I have to, I'll give up all rights to that sperm that's on file. I'll fight you tooth and nail to make sure that the life you ruin will be your own. You just think I'm supposed to sit around and just allow you to ruin my life?"

"Don't you still love me, Xay? I know that I haven't always been the best wife to you. I just want for us to be a family. I'll get rid of Chris, and you can tell that girl who's staying with you that it's over. Just come back to me, please?"

I didn't even bother to answer her. As far as I was concerned, we'd both contributed in some way to the demise of our marriage, and I wasn't going to sit there with Stacey and try to analyze what went wrong.

"Will you at least answer me? I hate it when you just

BEWARE OF DOG!

ignore me like that. Say something," Stacey demanded with
tears forming in her eyes. I just kept sitting there. I figured if I
just said absolutely nothing she'd finally leave.

I guess I wasn't thinking. I should have told Stacey to
maybe just leave because as I sat on the couch with my head
back and my eyes closed, I heard Stacey walk toward the
mantel. The next thing I know she picks up my night stick and
bashes in my thirty-two inch, flat-screen TV.

"What the hell is wrong with you? You are not going to
keep coming in here breaking up my shit."

"Go to hell, Xavier!" Stacey said as she walked to the
door, swung it open and walked out.

I knew Stacey wasn't dealing with a full deck these
days. Hell, a woman scorned is one crazy chick. I had no idea
what was coming next, but I knew that I had to cover my tracks.
I decided to call my captain and let him know what was going
on.

After my call with my captain, he suggested that I first
speak with my lawyer, so that's what I did. I called my lawyer,
the one that Troi had told me to call. My lawyer and the captain
both agreed that I should file a protection from abuse order
against Stacey. Now I know that I sound like a straight-up
punk, but as a police officer I have to protect my job. If I have
a domestic abuse charge against me, I automatically lose my
service weapon. Then comes the internal affairs investigation.
If I'm found guilty of a domestic abuse charge I can pretty
much hang up the idea of ever working in law enforcement.
I've seen it happen repeatedly on the police force. Men, not the
women, usually get the short end of the stick in these types of
situations. I wasn't going out like that. Call me what you like,
but call me employed.

I knew things were going to get ugly, but if I had it my

BEWARE OF DOG!

way, I was going to do everything in my power to remain professional on the job and be cordial to Stacey. At twelve, Justin was old enough to sense turmoil going on in the house. Ayanna, only two, only cared about watching Rolie Polie Olie and The Wiggles on television.

Once I filed the PFA, I figured I'd sit back and wait for the dust to start flying. It didn't take long before I received my first unknown call on my cell phone. I hesitated about answering it, because something told me it was Stacey.

"I can't believe you. You just stooped to an all-time low. You ain't shit," she said after I answered.

"Stacey, don't call me with this bullshit. You know you're not supposed to call, visit, write, nothing. Don't call me with this mess."

"You're going to pay for this, motherfucker. You can best believe that. If I don't do nothing else in life, I'm going to make sure you pay for this. And don't even think about coming to see your kids."

"Oh, so now you're going to use the kids to get back at me?"

"You're damn right. I told you not to fuck with me. This is just the beginning."

I simply hung up the phone. I called Stacey's mom. I figured she could talk some sense into her.

"Hey, Mom."

"How you doin', Xay? You don't even come over to see me no more. Where you been hiding these days?"

"Just trying to make that money, Mom. How are you feeling?"

"I can't complain, baby. I'm gettin' along."

"I hear that. I was calling to find out if you've talked to Stacey lately."

194

BEWARE OF DOG!

"Baby, the last time I spoke to Stacey, I hardly understood her. She was talkin' like she didn't have the sense God gave her. It's something wrong with that girl? She's got a lot of bitter feelings all bottled inside."

"Why do you say that?"

"I don't want to get involved with y'all's business. You know I don't like to meddle."

"I know, Ma, but if you could talk to her, I'd appreciate it. Like you said, Stacey isn't right. I know she's probably told you some of the things that are going on, but I just want to make sure that we both keep the children as the main priority, despite what's happening. All I care about is that their lives are not ruined by all of this mess."

"I hear you, baby. I've even tried to talk to Stacey, but like I said earlier, she's got all of this bitterness going on. I don't know if she's willing to listen just yet. You be patient though. I'm sure she'll come around."

"Alright, Ma. If you need anything, just give me a call. You've still got all of my numbers, right?"

"Yes, baby. If the kids come over, I'll make sure that I call you so you can stop by to see them. I love Stacey, she's my baby, but it's not right to keep a father away from his children. I didn't raise Stacey to be actin' like this."

"Thanks, Ma. I appreciate what you're doing for me. I know that I haven't been the best husband, but I love my children more than anything in this world."

"I know you do, baby. I'll talk to you later. Love you."

"Love you too, Ma."

Three days later, on Friday. Stacey dropped the kids off at her mother's so they could spend the night. True to her word, my mother-in-law called me and I stopped by to see the children. I was supposed to travel to Delaware with Troi, but

BEWARE OF DOG!

when my mother-in-law called, I dropped everything and ran over there. I dropped Troi off at her office since she said she had some work to catch up on and we were going to go out later on, after the kids went to bed.

Justin and Ayanna were so happy to see me, and Lord knows I was happy to see them too. Stacey wasn't due to come to pick up the kids until Saturday so my mother-in-law went upstairs and gave me the precious time alone with my children. Of course, Ayanna didn't want to get off of my lap and surprisingly, Justin, who is normally a quiet boy, wouldn't stop talking about all of the things that were going on with him, like the fact that this little girl, Raina, liked him and wanted Justin to meet her at the mall on Saturday evening. Justin was hoping that I could take him, but I explained to him that Mommy and I had to work some things out before I could take him and Ayanna to the mall. Finally, around 9:00 PM, Ayanna started dozing off, and Justin and I really got a chance to talk. I explained everything from my perspective, without speaking badly about Stacey. I didn't want my children to ever feel that the separation and divorce was their fault, and I didn't want them to take sides. Yeah, Stacey was acting a fool right about now, not letting me see my kids, but they didn't need to know that. If Stacey wasn't going to be rational, at least one of us had to be. Justin was a little sad, but as long as he knew it wasn't his fault or didn't feel stressed out about trying to get his mother and me back together, then I'd be alright. I knew that Ayanna was still young enough that she'd never really remember that I lived at home, so the way things were going to be would be a sense of normalcy for her. I just knew that I had to keep a close eye on Justin, especially at this age. In the long run, I wanted to fight Stacey for custody of the children. Children need their father just as much as they need their mother nowadays.

BEWARE OF DOG!

By the time I left my mother-in-law's it was 10:00 PM and Justin was even trying to nod off. I put Ayanna in her bed and tucked her in. She looked like such an angel sleeping. I kissed Justin on his head and peeked into my mother-in-law's room. She was barely awake.

"Thanks, Ma. I'm on my way out. If you need anything, just give me a call."

"Alright, baby. I'm glad you got to see your babies. Lock up for me. I'm so tired."

"Good night and thanks again, Ma."

I walked to my car feeling alive again. I knew that I hadn't been the best company for Troi lately, but now I was slowly coming out of the dumps. That is, until I got in my car—my other pride and joy, my 2002 Lincoln Navigator—to start it up, after a few seconds the engine turned over smoothly, the way that it always did. I picked up my cell phone to call Troi to let her know that I was on my way to pick her up, but then my engine made a loud noise, and then my car just turned off. I tried starting the engine again, but this time it just wouldn't turn over. I got out and lifted up the hood and looked at everything. It was all clean and shiny. Then, I remembered that my oil was due to be changed, but certainly it wasn't overdue. I pulled out the dip stick and noticed that my oil looked a little grainy. I don't know a hell of a lot about cars, but I know how to do the basics of changing my oil, my tires, my air filter and simple things like that, but I couldn't figure out why my car wouldn't start. As I walked back to the driver's side door, I noticed that my gas tank door was open. When I approached the tank door, I noticed it was all bent up and scratched, as if someone had pried it open. When I removed the gas cap, I saw a white substance all around the inside perimeter of the gas tank. I touched it and rubbed it between my fingers.

BEWARE OF DOG!

It sure as hell looked like sugar. It couldn't be. My cell phone rang and I noticed it was an unknown call. I picked up the phone.

"Hello."

"Hey, sweetie?" the unfamiliar voiced asked.

"Who the hell is this?"

"See how well you gon' be flossin' now in your broken-down ride," the unfamiliar voice stated and then hung up.

I called roadside assistance service and then called Troi to let her know that I'd be late and would just meet her at the apartment. As I waited for the tow truck, I decided to have a look around my ride and that's when I saw the word Cheater, spray painted for all of the world to see. As if things could get any worse, it began raining. I forgot meteorologists were calling for severe thunderstorms later in the day.

I called Fran, who's the manager at the Firestone garage and had the truck towed there. I placed the keys in the night drop box, but the tow truck driver warned me that his professional opinion was that the white substance was sugar. If what he said was true, then my Navigator was totally ruined. I knew that Stacey had turned out to be cruel, but this was just ridiculous. Thankfully, the tow truck driver was going my way, so he dropped me off at my apartment and when I got there, Troi was there. She was just what I needed to make me feel a little better. I was fuming and was contemplating my next move. Stacey would pay for this. But then, she was the mother of my children and I should just let all of this nonsense go, right?

"One should talk little and listen much."
—African proverb

Chapter 23

Corie

    I remember crying over an ex-boyfriend one time when I was sixteen years old. My mother saw me and was very upset that her only child was bothered.

    "What's wrong, child?"

    "Sean broke up with me."

    "Okay, so what's the problem? You still haven't told me why you're crying," my mother said in her deep Guyanese accent.

    "Because Sean broke up with me. He said that he needed some time and space to think things through. He didn't even have the decency to tell me face-to-face. He had the nerve to leave me a card."

    "Honey, let me explain to you a little golden rule I've set up for myself. I know it's easier said than done for me to tell you that these feelings will pass, because only you know what's in your heart, but as sure as I'm standing here right now, I can guarantee you that you'll get over this, and Sean will one day become a distant memory. You may even bump into him and you won't even remember ever feeling this way. Now, that's

BEWARE OF DOG!

not to say that you'll forget that he broke your heart, but I do promise you that you won't even remember the hurtful way you're feeling right now. Pain is only temporary. Be it physical or emotional, you just don't feel it the same way that you did forever."

"I just love him so much. I can't believe he did this to me. How could he do this to me?"

"Because he could. I know that you don't want to hear this right now, but you have to go through it to get through it. How do you think we grow? We do it by overcoming obstacles and dealing with adversities. Sean was no good for you anyway. I saw that from the start. He used you because you allowed him to."

"No he didn't!" I stated.

"You don't see it now, but I bet when he comes back your way, by then you'll be stronger and you'll see it."

"He said that he doesn't want to get back with me."

"Oh, he may say that now, but just remember this, they all come back," my mother stated.

"What do you mean?"

"I've dated a time or two in my day. Trust me when I tell you I haven't met a man that I dealt with who didn't come back in some way, shape or form. Now, he may not want to get back with you, but you can be rest assured that he'll call, write or even send a friend, but he'll want to know how you made out. There's nothing written on what I'm telling you that I know of, but that's just been my experience. They all come back! And when he does, you'll be so much stronger by then. You'll hardly remember feeling this way. Mark my words," Mom stated.

True to her words. The summer after that whole Sean fiasco, I got a call from him out of the clear blue and he wanted

200

BEWARE OF DOG!

to know how I was doing and if he could take me out. I even
decided that he could after a few phone calls, but then when I
saw him, my mother was correct, I didn't even see him in the
same light anymore. Somehow, his teeth weren't straight
enough, I didn't like the way that he wore his hair and he was
suddenly too short for me. He hadn't changed his appearance at
all, but I just saw him differently.

With all that said, I was ready to go back to the club. I
began my first night, with Lance following closely. Overall, it
had been close to two-and-a-half months since I had worked in
the club at full capacity. The college students were already back
to school, thankfully, my Temple students were a loyal bunch of
partygoers, so I knew that I had to throw an all-night jam for
them. I wanted all of the black Greek fraternity and sororities
in the house. Vanita, Lance and I were thinking of ways to set
up a stage so we could have a Greek step show and possibly
award prizes to the winners. I knew with the right publicity, we
would have the place jam packed.

I really didn't want a whole bunch of college folks in
there, but my Temple and Cheyney students were a dedicated
bunch and they really weren't in to that blunt smoking and all of
that other crazy nonsense. It had taken two weeks to get the
club fixed up to cater the large crowd that we expected. We
called Design Shooters on South Street and they hooked us up
with the most awesome flyers. Lance had taken care of hiring a
few guys who were down on their luck to hand out the flyers
and place larger ones in various stores and restaurants around
the city and up on the two campuses, so the word was out. We
decided to sell advance tickets, so the night before the show, we
had sold more than three hundred tickets and admission would
be more at the door. Thankfully, the basement that I had
renovated was all ready for operation and it was equipped with

BEWARE OF DOG!

a live jazz room and a "living" room where some of the folks who wanted to get on the mic and kick a little spoken word could do so without all of the noise from the club. I even hired my cousin, Mark, who was going to represent on the mic with his revolutionary style poems.

I was pumped that things were slowly getting back to the way things used to be. The threats had ceased entirely, and I noticed that my life was getting back to some sort of normalcy. Lance had even had lunch with Troi for a recommendation for a good divorce attorney. The separation papers had been issued and that's when all hell broke loose.

The night of the step show, the club was jam packed. I even saw Rashan in the club. I started to have his ass kicked out, but he came over and asked if we could bury the hatchet. I wasn't sure if I could trust him, but he seemed sincere. I was still going to keep my eye on him.

Poor Vanita was running around like a chicken with its head cut off, and I had made a mental note that she deserved a raise after all that I had put her through. I mean, she was doing her job, but she was truly going the distance, and I was thankful for her services. Lance was also putting in his time since he had a few more hours in the day and although we were both working like crazy to ensure that things got done, we were both enjoying the idea that we worked well together. We weren't doing the mushy, googly-eyed stuff, but we did have a special bond, and I was actually beginning to soften up a bit. By 11:00 PM, the Temple students were representing. We had placed special advertisements on WDAS FM AND WHAT AM. The infamous Al Butler and Dave Warren from WHAT AM and the Acres of Diamond Experience had come in to help us host the throw down, and they were airing the party live on their show. Anybody who listens to their show on Saturdays, from 6:00 PM

BEWARE OF DOG!

to 10:00 PM, knows how much energy they can bring to a party. Dave and Al had put out the word that any students who wore their school's or Greek's paraphernalia would receive non-alcoholic discounted drink specials. It was a ploy that worked all too well. The entire scene reminded me of a one from School Daze. It was so much dog barking, skeeweeing, and oo-ooping going on that I thought I was going to lose my mind. You know since a sista is a Delta, I had to represent, too, looking all too good in my crimson and cream. A couple of the AKAs were up in there like they were trying to take over with their little dances, so you know I had to get up there and do a little old-school stepping once my younger sorors were done. You know we shut 'em down. After I got off stage, I was feeling too good. I figured I'd let the younguns do their thang.

It was close to 3:00 AM by the time Vanita and I finally got everyone out of the club. I was so tired and you couldn't tell me that my feet weren't bleeding. I realized that I hadn't seen Lance for about an hour. Knowing him, he was probably upstairs writing out bills and tallying up all of the expenses for the night's events. I missed my sweetie, besides I couldn't think of a better excuse for us to do a little catching up ourselves, than in my office, on the floor, butt-naked, laying on a heap of money. I tried hitting him on the two-way so that he could be prepared to service a sista's needs because I was horny as all get-out, but I didn't get an answer. I got up to my office, the door was locked. I searched for my key, and when I opened the door, the light was off. I figured Lance was on the same page as me. Who knew? I guess I wasn't quite thinking. I stepped inside of the darkness and that's when I got this cold chill that ran up my spine. I just knew there was going to be some trouble. When I reached for the light, I felt an unfamiliar hand on mine.

BEWARE OF DOG!

"What the fuck," I began.

Suddenly, I was pulled in and I felt the all-too-familiar cold steel up against my head.

"I wish you would move. I'll blow you fucking head off, bitch! Today is the day. I've given you several chances, but now you're going to pay."

It was still dark inside, but my eyes were beginning to focus. That's when I noticed Lance sitting on the couch.

"Get over on there with that motherfucker. Both of you sons of bitches are going to pay."

I hesitated for a moment. I wasn't going to be too many more bitches and motherfuckers. "Who the hell..." I began as I was hit in the back of the head with the butt of the gun. I just knew I was about to black out.

"Get your ass over there, I said."

I stumbled to the couch and took my place beside Lance.

"You two think you're so fucking slick. I tried and tried to turn my head to this bullshit. How long do you think a woman can take this shit? He's my fucking husband, but you just wouldn't leave well enough alone!" Sherrie stated.

"Sherrie, you're being ridiculous. You know damn well that you and I are not like that," Lance stated.

"What the hell do you mean? We're not like that? What the fuck is that? Are you forgetting that we're married? You're my damn husband, but I've got to make a damn appointment just to get your ass to come home."

"Sherrie, you know that I don't love you. Keep it real, you don't even love me. We're just together for convenience."

"See what I mean. For years, we were fine. Yeah, I knew that you were doing your thang, but you never loved any of those bitches. Now, you've up and just left me. You can't just walk out on me for this fucking slut. This fucking home

BEWARE
OF
DOG!

wrecker. She's not even made from anything. She owns a fucking ghetto club for heaven's sake. What are all of my friends going to think?" Sherrie stated, waving the gun in the air.

"I don't give a damn what your bourgeois friends think. I've gotta be happy for me," Lance said.

"See, that's what I mean. You used to care. Your father can't even talk any sense into you."

"Fuck that. I'm my own damn man. I'm tired of living a damn lie. You know you've never loved me. You never even wanted me. You just love the damn money and prestige that goes along with it. Keep it real," Lance stated, standing.

"Sit the hell down. Sit down!" Sherrie said, rising up from behind my desk.

"What are you going to do? I know damn well that you ain't going to fire that damn gun, hell, you wouldn't because you would mess up your most precious manicure," Lance said.

"I'm warning you, sit down," Sherrie stated as she aimed the gun at me.

"Sit down, Lance," I stated, not knowing how far this crazy-ass woman would go. Lance backed off.

Sherrie then relaxed a bit and sat back down. She began mumbling something under her breath and rocking back and forth, holding herself tightly. "So, answer me this one question. It's over between us, huh?" Sherrie asked.

"Sherrie, you're intelligent, pretty and you have a bright future ahead of you. You're involved with all of those prestigious organizations. You'll have no problem meeting someone who will love you the way that you need to be loved. I'm just not that man. I can't deny my own feelings anymore."

Sherrie looked as if she had lost it. Her eyes turned glassy, as if she had gone to a far-away place. While she was

BEWARE OF DOG!

still seated behind the desk, with the gun pointed in our direction, Sherrie went into her Louis Vutton hand bag and poured something on the floor. I was thinking, I know this heifer ain't wasting no damn soda on my plush carpet. Oh no she didn't. Suddenly, Sherrie stood. With her left hand, she held a lighter. She bent down to light something, while she placed the gun on the desk. Instantly, she was engulfed in flames. "If I can't have you, I don't want to live anymore!."

"Omigod! That's gasoline," I said.

I scrambled to get some blankets or look for something to put out the flames. Lance jumped over the desk and tried to cover Sherrie with his body, which caused them to fall to the floor. Papers began burning and next thing I knew, my entire office was up in flames, but thankfully, the sprinklers came on and the smoke detector began blaring. The smoke was so thick, I thought my lungs were going to collapse from the burning and stinging I felt in my chest. I ran to the window and pulled it up, gasping for air. I felt an intense heat all over my body and I was forced to climb out of the window and onto the fire escape. I ran down the steps like never before. In the distance I could hear the fire engines, and all I could think about was Lance and I felt horrible for leaving him behind, but I had to get out. I got to the bottom of the stairs and realized that I would have to jump, but thank God for me, there was a black Suburban that was parked underneath so I jumped on the hood. There was a man behind the wheel and I think I must have scared him to death, but at least I'd be alive to attend his funeral. He got out of the car and I almost fell on the ground from shock. It was Jarvis, my son Tori's father.

"Jarvis, what the hell are you doing here? In the alley."

"Why the hell are you jumping on the hood of my car?"

"How about a fire is going on upstairs."

BEWARE OF DOG!

Just then Lance called out my name from the top of the stairs and when I looked up, he waved at me to let me know that he was okay. My heart skipped a beat of relief.

"Lance, thank God."

"Fuck!" Jarvis stated.

"I'm on my way down," Lance stated.

Suddenly, Jarvis took a step forward and grabbed my arm. "Get in the truck," he demanded.

"Let go of me. What the hell are you doing?" I asked.

"I told you before, I can't live without you. Now get in the car. You ruined my life, now I'm going to ruin yours. Don't get homie fucked up," Jarvis warned.

After all I had been through, I knew there was no way that I was going to get in that truck with Jarvis. He was about to get his ass kicked and I mean for real. Did he know that my club was burning down? Sherrie tried to set my ass ablaze and now he was talking some ole Fatal Attraction shit. Somebody better warn this brotha.

I looked at my arm, then looked back up at Jarvis. Meanwhile, I could hear Lance approaching us. I knew what was coming next, or at least I figured what was coming and I wasn't about to wait around to read Lance's and my obituary. I put my kickboxing moves on Jarvis's ass. I took my left fist and pushed it upward in his nose, causing it to break instantly. I learned this move from Gunnie, my personal trainer and the best kickboxing instructor in Delaware. I then grabbed both of Jarvis's shoulders and pulled him into me and brought my right knee forcefully up in his stomach. When Jarvis doubled over in pain, I kicked him one last time for good measure. By that time Lance was down the steps and coughing uncontrollably. Thankfully, the sirens were pulling up around the corner. I ran to the end of the alley and called a fire woman.

BEWARE OF DOG!

"Here, here. I need an ambulance."

The EMTs came back in the alley and gave Lance some oxygen and then I noticed that Jarvis was still squirming around on the ground. The EMTs began working on his bloody nose, so I slipped around to the police officer and told them what happened and they arrested his ass right on the spot.

As it turned out, when they searched his car, he had two handguns in the glove box, duct tape, rope and several knives. They also found a note in the truck, explaining why he killed me and information about his suicide. Apparently, Jarvis wanted us both to die since our son, Tori, had died all those years ago. When Lance got a good look at Jarvis, he mentioned that he was the same homeless guy that he spoke to at Bluezette who was telling him how he lost his family several years ago, but that soon, he would be reunited with them all. At last, I had found out who had been stalking me. God only knows how Jarvis had intended on killing me.

Thankfully, Lance was okay. He suffered minor burns to his hand and smelled like Smokey the Bandit, but otherwise he'd be okay. With Jarvis arrested, all we had to worry about was making sure Sherrie would be okay and then all of the drama would be over, right?

"Every good bye ain't good night."
—Author unknown

Chapter 24

Troi

I knew things were bad for Malcolm, but never in a
million years did I think it would go down like it did. Malcolm
had been a part of my life for so long that I could barely
remember life without him. But in the end, he took care of me
and represented well. It was just a shame that it was way too
late for us.

I had been living from pillar to post since the day that I
was on the run. Thankfully for me, I have an office equipped
with a bathroom, because I had all but moved in there. I
refused to go back to my house, and I didn't want to take that
mess up to my parents' home. At first turning to Xavier was out
of the question because he was going through his own damn
drama, and after the way his wife performed that day, I figured
I'd give him some time and space to sort out that whole mess.
Besides, I had my own drama and I didn't want him to get
involved in my mess any more than he had already. But when I
called to let him know that I would be staying with friends in
New Jersey he convinced me that he needed me more than ever.
He explained to me about the protection from abuse order that

BEWARE
OF
DOG!

he filed against Stacey and at least that let me know that he was serious about the two of us not playing that "other woman/man" game. I hadn't been able to get in touch with Corie because she was trying to reclaim her life, too, in Guyana, so I kept her updated with my life through voicemail messages while she was away. I really didn't want to tell her too much because she was supposed to be relaxing, not worrying over my problems.

When Xavier told me about Stacey being gay, I almost fell over. I finally confided in him about what was really going on between Malcolm and me and we had to laugh at the whole situation. How ironic was that? I mean two people who were actually left by their significant others for the same sex. The whole story could have made a best-selling novel. What was strange is that it actually brought us closer together.

It was Friday morning, almost a week since I had seen Malcolm. When my secretary walked in my office and told me there were two detectives waiting in the lobby to speak to me, I almost wished that I had a glass of wine to smooth over the edges. I just felt it in my bones that the news wasn't going to be good. Aside from that, my right eye had been twitching for three days straight and that always signaled bad news for me.

Debra showed the detectives in, and I looked at the woman first and then the man, hoping that I could get a feel for why they were actually there.

"Ms. Stokes, I'm Detective Mayock and this is my partner, Detective Carter," the female officer said.

"Good to meet you. Please, have a seat," I stated.

"Ms. Stokes, I'm sorry to have to tell you this, but there is no easy way to say this."

"Just say it. I know it's about Malcolm. Is he dead?" I asked, fearing the worse.

"Ma'am, we're going to have to ask you to come down

BEWARE
OF
DOG!

to the morgue to view a body. We believe it may be your fiancé," Detective Carter stated.

All I could think was, This guy must have to do this all of the time. He just blurted that out.

"Ms. Stokes, are you alright? Would you like to have a seat?" Detective Mayock stated.

"No, I'm alright. Just let me get something to drink and tell my secretary that I'm leaving."

"Ma'am, are you alright?" Detective Carter asked again.

"I'll be fine. I'm okay," I stated. I couldn't figure out for the life of me why I was taking it so calmly. Was I human? Didn't I love Malcolm? Why wasn't I falling apart like I was supposed to? All I could really think was, Is all of this mess over now? Are those guys still going to come after me?

When we arrived at the city morgue, I had to brace myself. It wasn't every day that I got to see a dead person, especially not my fiancé. When the city examiner pulled the sheet back, I gasped for air. I was surprised, but it wasn't Malcolm. The guy looked a lot like Malcolm and had on the engraved bracelet that I had given to Malcolm for his birthday last year, but it wasn't Malcolm. In fact, it was Tremaine or Steve, one of the guys from the videotape, but I wasn't sure which one. I was sure that it was one of the brutes who had been chasing me that day outside of the bank. How could I ever forget them?

"That's not him."

"Are you sure, ma'am?" Detective Mayock asked.

"Detective Mayock, I think I know what my fiancé looks like, and this man is not him."

"Sorry, ma'am. We just thought..."

All of a sudden, I felt my breakfast creeping up in my throat and I had to get out of there and get some air.

BEWARE OF DOG!

"Wait. We'll take you back to your office. Do you need a ride?" Detective Mayock asked as I ran for the exit.

"I'll be fine. I'll catch a cab," I said through clenched teeth.

When I got outside, I leaned up against the wall and prayed my breakfast would go back down to my stomach where it belonged. As I continued leaning up against the building, I closed my eyes and tried to figure out exactly what was going on.

"Psst. Psst. Troi, come over here."

"What. Malcolm?" I asked to the guy who sounded a lot like Malcolm but looked like a homeless man pushing an old shopping cart.

"Just act like you're going in your bag to get me some change."

"What the hell is going on?"

"Just do what I say," he instructed.

As I searched my bag slowly, Malcolm began explaining.

"Troi, please believe me when I tell you that I love you."

I stopped looking in the bag and gave him a "screw you" look.

"I know you don't believe me, but please just hear me out. I have about ten minutes and then I've got to go. I'm in a lot of trouble. I need you to go back in there and tell them that you made a mistake and that the man laying in there is me."

"What? You want me to lie and possibly risk my entire career?"

"It won't be a lie if you don't do it."

"Is that a threat, Malcolm?"

"All I'm saying is that I will be laying in there and you will have to identify the body sooner or later. Please. I need for

BEWARE
OF
DOG!

you to collect the insurance money that I took out on myself.
It's a one million dollar policy. When a guy by the name of
Louie comes for the money, write him a check for $250,000 and
that's all you'll have to do."

"And if I don't?"

"Who do you have to identify both of our bodies?
Listen, then take $200,000 and give Corie back her money that I
stole from her. Take the rest and invest it or do whatever you
want with it and know that I'll always love you. The whole
ordeal with the tape will be over and everything. I'm so sorry
for all of this that I brought to you."

"Who was that guy in the morgue? Wasn't that the guy
from the tape?"

"Yeah, it was him. I doubt they'll ever find Steve's
body," Malcolm said.

"Who is this Louie fellow?"

"You're asking way too many questions. Aren't you
supposed to be a woman of the law? The less you know the
better."

"Tell me now!" I demanded.

"Let's just say that Louie took care of things. Now, I
need to pay him the money that he's owed. You know those
fucking faggots had the nerve to take the money that I gathered
and then wanted to back out of our deal and go to the press
anyway. They had to be dealt with. That's why I need this
money. Then this nightmare will be all over. Got that now? You
deserve happiness with that guy you've been staying with."

"What! You know about him? How?"

"I've been keeping my eye on you. Don't worry, I'm
not mad. In a weird way I was glad that dude was there to
make sure that nobody hurt you. I would have killed myself if
something would have happened to you. I've gotta run. It's not

213

safe for me in this country right now. Who knows, maybe in a year or so I'll be able to come back home."

"Where are you going?"

"I don't want to tell you, but I may try your home place. Maybe when I get back in town I'll look you up. Hopefully you won't be married by then."

"Malcolm, I think you need to stay focused on what's in front of us now and not worry about my future."

"You're right. Let me get out of here. Don't tell a soul what I've just told you. It could land both of us in jail or in the morgue.

"Here, take this dollar."

"Why?" I asked.

"You've just become my attorney. Hopefully you'll respect the attorney-client privilege in this matter."

"Malcolm, don't try to play lawyer with me. You wouldn't know the law if I sat down and wrote it out for you."

I took the dollar from Malcolm and he sauntered off.

"I stood there for a few seconds and tried to prepare myself to go back inside of the medical examiner's office and commit perjury. I was making the correct choice. I mean after all, this was going to stop all of the drama from further escalating, right?

BEWARE OF DOG!

"If you always do what you always did than you'll always get what you've always gotten."
—Author unknown

Chapter 25

Xavier

I don't care if it takes me the rest of my life to get my shit together, at least I'm on the road to recovery right now. As painful as it was, I had broken things off with Troi. I'm trying to be real to myself for once in my life. My whole life has been nothing but drama and I just wanted out. Now, that's not to say that I never, ever wanted to see Troi again, and who knows what the future may hold for us, but right now, the way I see it, we needed to just take a moment and get our own personal affairs in order.

For me, the breaking point was my ride. Now everyone who knows me, knows that my Navigator is my pride and joy. You see, Stacey is one smart bitch. I hate referring to a woman that way and my parents didn't raise me to be disrespecting a woman, but do you know that the entire ordeal with the sugar in the tank was a calculated mess. Of course I was upset about my ride, but when I called the car insurance company, I damn near flipped my lid when they told me that my wife had called earlier in the day to cancel our car insurance policy. So, you know

BEWARE OF DOG!

what that means? Under normal circumstances, my car would have been covered under vandalism and they would have to just replace it or whatever they do when shit like this occurs. But, Stacey played herself and thank God for me, the customer service representative had entered the wrong policy number when she attempted to cancel my policy. So, thankfully, on a technicality, my insurance was still in good standing. Now you know I called and cussed that bitch out, right? You can tell she was so mad, that she vowed to "get me." So, I had to move to plan B, which would cause me a bit of stress and confusion, but I had to reclaim my life.

First thing that I did was I spoke to the children. I explained to them that their daddy wouldn't be seeing them for a while. Justin was upset and he thought it was his fault, like he had done something to cause me to not want to see him for awhile. I had to reassure my little man that I loved him more than anything in this world and that nothing would ever come between us.

The next thing that I decided to do was to move and not let anyone who knew both Stacey and me know where I'd be going. It was going to cost me a nice little grip, because I had to find a place that had a garage for me to keep my new truck. There was no way that I was going to go out like that again.

The hardest part was when I called Troi and told her that I needed to speak with her.

She came over to the apartment and she looked tired as hell.

"Troi, I really need to talk with you."

"This sounds serious. What's up?"

"I'm just gon' say it. I need some time and space to get myself together. Right now, I'm going through so damn much with Stacey, and shit is going to get a whole lot worse before it

216

BEWARE OF DOG!

gets any better. I've put you and Stacey through so much that I don't want to even be the same person that I was before. You definitely deserve better and then again, so do I."

"You know, if you would have said all of this about two weeks ago, I just might have been upset, but with all of the drama that's going on in my life right now, I have to admit, you're absolutely right. We both deserve more, and this is no way to start off a relationship. It'd be doomed from the start. Who knows what the future will hold, but right now, I've got to get myself together too. Malcolm died last night."

"Oh, baby, I'm so sorry. Here I am talking about us not seeing each other anymore and now this?"

"One has nothing to do with the other. Going our separate ways is inevitable. I'll be fine. I just hope that we can still be friends. I'm here for you if you need me. I know you have your own stuff you're going through and putting both of our crap together would be crazy. I need to go. I have to get over to the hotel and let Corie know what's going on. I have a million things to take care of."

"Here I am hitting you with all of this shit and now is obviously not the time to have this discussion. You need me to go with you?" I asked.

"No, but I'll call you later. I need to sit and talk with my best friend right now."

I kissed Troi on her forehead and told her I'd speak with her soon. Breaking up with her was the right thing to do, right?

BEWARE OF DOG!

"Silence can be louder than words."
—Author unknown

Chapter 26

Corie

Life has a strange way of redirecting your path. I thought it best not to attend Sherrie's funeral when her family was going to have her service in a few days. I stayed at the Ritz and awaited Lance's return from the hospital. The fire commissioner said that although Sherrie was able to climb onto the fire escape, she had suffered third-degree burns on seventy-five percent of her body. Now, I was injured on my thigh once from some water that burned through my Styrofoam cup and trust me when I tell you that I had to go to the emergency room and that was only a second-degree burn. I don't even want to imagine the type of pain Sherrie must have been going through. Of course I was feeling like shit because I was blaming myself for contributing to her resorting to killing herself. Lance kept assuring me that it wasn't my fault, but then I had to think about things logically. If I hadn't been involved with this married man, then maybe, just maybe his wife wouldn't have resorted to this.

Lance confided in me one night while we were at his place that Sherrie suffered from bipolar disorder and from

BEWARE OF DOG!

schizophrenic episodes and the family was adamant about not ruining the family name and not having her committed. So Lance was damn near ordered to stay and get his wife the mental treatment she needed. The family had done an excellent job about not letting anyone know what was going on. Despite all of that information, I still felt like shit. I was moping around the suite and then the doorman called me downstairs and gave me some fantastic news. My best friend was on her way up to see me. I could hardly wait, so I ran to the door to await Troi's arrival. When she got off the elevator I just started running to her. In all fairness, I should have turned to her when I was going through all of this, but I just didn't want to complicate things between us and I, especially since I found out that Malcolm had been stealing money from me.

"Girl, I'm so glad to see you!" I said, running up and almost knocking Troi down.

"Me too. So much has been going on. I'm just glad that this drama is over for me. If it's not, well too bad, because it is now. I'm putting a stop to all of this crap that's going on in my life."

"I hear you. I need to come up out of this suite and reclaim my life. What are you doing up here?"

"I came to see my best friend. And to give you this," Troi said, handing me a check for two hundred thousand dollars, from her personal checking account.

"Troi, no. This is not your problem to fix. This is between Malcolm and me. When I see him, I'll make sure he gives me my money."

"Stop. Malcolm is dead."

"What?" I said, not believing my ears.

"It happened yesterday afternoon."

"Wait a minute. I spoke with you yesterday and you

never mentioned this."

"Girl, you and I both have so much drama going on that I just didn't have time to call you back. I knew you were going to need to be there for Lance so I figured I'd come today."

"Damn. How are you doing? Do you need anything? What happened?" I asked, leading us back to the suite.

"Surprisingly, I'm doing alright. Malcolm got shot. Probably those thugs who were after him," Troi explained. I knew Troi better than I knew myself, and I knew she wasn't telling me everything.

"Troi, what aren't you telling me?"

"Do me a favor, don't ask. Everything ain't for everybody to know."

"Enough said. If you need me, you know the rest."

"That's why I came here. Before I have to face the rest of the world."

"Have you told Malcolm's parents yet?"

"Yeah. I went over there last night after I found out and told them. Malcolm's mom was damn near in a coma when I left this morning. That's another reason why I didn't call you last night," Troi stated.

"I'm surprised you're not upset beyond control," I said, eyeing Troi closely.

"I'll be alright. I've just got a lot on my mind and I'm still trying to put all of this together so that it makes sense to me," Troi stated.

"Well, you can say what you want, but I know you and that's all that I'm saying."

"That would be the first time. Listen, I've got to run. I'm going to have Malcolm cremated."

"Really? You know black folks don't normally go for that kind of stuff."

BEWARE OF DOG!

"Well, this one is going for it. I think a cremation is easier to deal with than a funeral service."

"How do you think Malcolm's mom is going to feel about that?"

"I can't worry about it. I've got to do what's best for me. He had me listed as the next of kin," Troi stated.

"I hear ya."

"I'll call you when I know more details about the service," Troi said before leaving.

I was so tense after Troi left, and I knew that the only thing that would make me feel better was to go and work out and then get me a massage from the spa. I got dressed and was heading out the door when my cell phone rang. I thought about not answering it, but then I figured that it might be Lance. I looked at the Caller I.D., but didn't recognize the number. I knew there was no way that I was answering it after all I had been through with Jarvis and his nonsense. Whoever it was left a message and when I checked, it was Merwin Andrews, a colleague who had been on my case about selling him my club. I had always blown him off when he called with his lucrative proposal, but this time I had to sit and think for a few minutes. I had all but made up my mind when Lance walked in.

"What are you doing just sitting there?"

"Thinking, baby. How are you feeling?"

"Tired. The meeting was fine, but then afterward, the shit hit the fan."

"What happened?"

"Just a bunch of finger pointing. Sherrie's family trying to place blame, knowing that she was suffering from a mental illness all along, but wouldn't allow anyone to help her for fear that their precious society friends would find out. What are you up to?" Lance asked.

BEWARE OF DOG!

"I'm sitting here thinking. I got a call from Merwin. He wants to buy the club."

"What's new about that? Merwin is always trying to get you to sell to him."

"Yeah, but this time I'm really thinking about it. I'm in desperate need of a change. I'd love to get away and start anew."

"Where do you want to go?"

"I don't know. I'm still thinking about it all."

"You know, Nassau is a nice place to start. That is if the invitation is open to me too."

"Of course. I was sitting here thinking what would it take for you to leave Philly and come with me."

"Not much, if you'd marry me."

"What? We can't talk about something like this. After all, your wife did just pass away."

"You know as well as I that it's sad what happened to Sherrie. You know I love you and what Sherrie and I had has been over for years. You act as if you're afraid to show me your true feelings. You don't always have to be so hard, you know."

"Yeah, I do. That's what makes me who I am."

"You didn't answer my question. Would you marry me? I'm not asking you to marry me right now but I want to know what would you say if I ask you again in another six months or so?"

"Lance, you know I have so much love for you and we make a wonderful team, but marriage is not for me," I stated.

"Corie, I love you and I want to spend the rest of my life with you."

"I feel the same way that you do, but why do we need to get married in order to spend the rest of our lives together? It's

BEWARE
OF
DOG!

not like marriage is going to mysteriously cement that union. I just don't get the hype over marriage anyway. It's so overrated. What we have works well for me."

"It does for me too. I just want you to know that it's not going to be so easy to get rid of me. I want the whole world to know that we belong to each other."

"Not for nothing, Lance, but isn't that the same sentiment that you shared with Sherrie? And then came me."

"No. Sherrie and I were never in love and I've told you a million and one times that our marriage was for convenience. Our parents ran that show," Lance explained.

"But what about the millions of couples who get married each year, truly believing that theirs is a marriage that will really last forever and that there is no one in the world who could ever come between them? Next thing you know, they're headed for divorce court," I stated.

"I can't speak for them. All I know is how I feel right here and now. I love you and that's all I know today. I can't make promises for tomorrow, except I'll try with all of my heart to love you the way that I want to be loved. I can't guarantee anything other than that," Lance stated.

"That's all that I desire then. Nothing but your very best will do. You can keep all of that other stuff."

"I still want you to marry me."

"We'll see. Let's call Merwin back and see what he's talking about before we go running down the damn aisle."

While I called Merwin, Lance told me he had to run out to the store. I called Merwin and of course he tried to insult me by offering me $250,000 for my club. He and I both knew that it was worth two times that amount. Finally, after a tough negotiation, Merwin offered me $425,000 and I accepted. Just as I was hanging up the phone, Lance came strolling in like he had just hit the jackpot.

"It looks like we need to start researching some property sites in Nassau," I said.

"Merwin offered you a good deal?"

"It's good enough. What's up with you? Why are you showing your thirty-twos?"

"Let's go out to dinner," Lance stated.

"Lance, do you think that's a good idea? I mean you haven't even buried your wife yet. What if your parents' friends see you."

"I told you. That relationship with Sherrie was over a long time ago. I don't give a damn what people think. I want to go out to dinner with my baby. Now get dressed."

"Lance, you know I rarely give a damn what people think about me, but this time, let's just stay in and order some dinner. I don't want to have to curse one of your parents' bourgeois friends out."

"Fine. I wanted to give you this over a candlelight dinner," Lance said, kneeling down in front of me and pulling out a black velvet box.

"What's this?"

"It's a pre-engagement ring. Open it."

I opened the box and saw a diamond bigger than New York City looking back at me. It was canary yellow in a princess cut and it had to be all of ten carats.

"Lance, I can't accept this," I stated.

"Why the hell not?"

"I thought we agreed that there would be no marriage right now."

"Did I say anything about marriage? I told you this is a pre-engagement ring."

"Well if this is the pre-engagement ring, I'd love to see

BEWARE OF DOG!

the engagement ring. What, you're going to get me the state of California next time?"

"If that's what you want. Only the best for my baby. All jokes aside, all that I've put you through with this whole madness with Sherrie, you deserve this. I'm just really serious about showing you how much you mean to me. If I have to spend the rest of my life trying to get you to marry me then that's what I'll do. Now, please put this ring on and promise me that you'll always be there for me."

I slid the ring on my finger and couldn't help but admire its beauty. I kissed Lance and looked at him sideways. Yeah, just maybe I could get used to coming home to him every night. Although I had been against the whole concept of marriage, love and happiness, maybe, just maybe I could get used to all of this. After all, Lance was my dream man, right?

"Every closed eye ain't shut."
—Author Unknown

Chapter 27

Xavier

    So, just like that, Troi and I decided that we were going to call it quits. Troi was a beautiful woman, and in my own way I had mad love for her, but truth be told, we should have never gone down that road in the first place. But since it happened, I had to learn something from the mistakes that I made and I had to move on with my life and realize that perhaps this whole thing with Troi happened so that I could face reality that Stacey and I should have never married in the first place. But again, since we did and we had two beautiful children together, we just needed to both be mature enough to raise our children. I knew that Stacey was way too bitter for me to have a cordial conversation with her.

    One night, as I was packing my belongings for my move to my new town house, I was watching the news and the Fraternal Order of Police were having their annual awards ceremony and who do I see all decked out but Stacey walking alongside Chris. She had this fake-ass smile on and was looking directly into the camera as if she knew that I'd be watching, like "hey, Xay, fuck you too." I had to laugh because

the joke would be on Chris. They deserved each other. Stacey looked as if she was about four months pregnant. Now ain't that some shit.

When I moved into my new town house, I'm not going to lie and tell you that I wasn't lonely as hell in the beginning. This was the first time in my life that I wasn't all up in some woman's face, and although I had a few ladies trying to holla at me, I just wasn't up for all of that. I was even going to try the celibate thing. I was dying to see my kids, but for the moment, I just had to be satisfied with speaking to them on the phone. I wanted to wait until the divorce hearing so that I could let a judge determine how and when I'd see them. I had made sure that I purchased a three-bedroom house so that Ayanna and Justin would each have their own rooms. I'd have to wait to see what the outcome was going to be with this baby.

The divorce hearing was scheduled and I sought the counsel of an attorney, Ruth Jawinski, whom Troi had recommended. She was an older white woman, but her reputation was flawless in family law. I was so nervous on the day of the court hearing. Stacey sauntered in with this broken down attorney who looked like he had seen better days when he wasn't drinking. My attorney assured me that I wouldn't have to pay more than twelve hundred dollars per month and that I'd at least have visitation every other weekend. The judge was a black woman who looked stern, but fair. I was so damn nervous having to sit   in front of this judge, which was odd since I had testified as a police officer, probably more than two hundred times. But this was different. I knew that my life with my children and the time that I spent with them was determined because of the possible lies that Stacey would profess. Since Stacey was the petitioner, her attorney was allowed to go first.

"You honor, my client would like for you to a grant

divorce between herself and Mr. DeVoe. My client would like to waive her right to custody of the two children. She'd like Mr. DeVoe to raise the children, Justin, twelve, and Ayanna, two.

"What!" I exploded.

"Mr. DeVoe, I'll remind you that you're in a court of law," the judge advised.

"I apologize for my client's outburst, Your Honor. May we have a fifteen minute recess, Your Honor? This is surprising news to my client," my lawyer said.

"Court will resume in fifteen minutes."

When I looked over at Stacey, she gave me this sneaky little smirk. Of course I was the happiest man on the planet. Hell yeah, I wanted the children, but never in a million years did I think that Stacey would say that she wanted me to raise them. But, I knew that I couldn't show my happiness to Stacey, so I just gave her this mean-ass look, like I was disappointed in her yet again. Stacey got up to go to the bathroom, rubbing her protruding belly and she made a comment to me.

"See what your dumb ass is going to do now with two kids. Now you're going to see just how hard this shit really is. You played yourself, asshole."

For some reason, I just didn't see it that way. I saw it as a way to stay close my children and yet, I couldn't understand for the life of me how Stacey thought that this was a punishment. I conferred with my lawyer and told him that I'd be elated if I could raise my kids, but what about the baby? The way that I looked at it, Stacey could keep the baby as long as I had Justin and Ayanna I was cool.

"All rise. Court is in session. Judge Patricia Smalls residing," the bailiff stated, after we returned from recess.

"Mr. Appel, is your client aware that she is giving away

full custodial rights to Mr. DeVoe?"

"Yes she is, Your Honor. Mrs. DeVoe would like for Mr. DeVoe to raise the children."

"All right," the judge stated.

"Ms. Jawinski, you may present your argument," the judge said.

"Your honor, Mr. DeVoe would honor the request by Mrs. DeVoe to have full custody of their children," my lawyer said.

"On the matter of divorce, I hear by grant the divorce between Mr. and Mrs. DeVoe. In regard to the custody of their two children, I hereby grant full custodial rights to Mr. DeVoe. Mr. DeVoe you will be awarded twelve hundred dollars per month, child support."

"What!" Stacey yelled.

"Mrs. DeVoe, what did you expect? You were asked twice if you understood the rights that you were giving to Mr. DeVoe," Judge Smalls stated.

"I'm not paying his cheating ass a red cent."

"Mrs. DeVoe! You're out of line. Use that type of profanity in my courtroom again and I'll hold you in contempt. Now sit down!" the judge demanded.

"Why do I have to pay him? He's the one who was cheating on me," Stacey continued to yell.

"Mrs. DeVoe, I'm warning you. Sit down or you'll be spending a few days in jail."

"Well, y'all need to arrest me now because I'll be damn if he's going to get away with this shit. This cheating bastard has all but ruined my life and now this is how it's going down. You're going to pay for this, bitch!" Stacey yelled.

"Get her out of here!" the judge yelled to the bailiff.

"I hate you, Xavier! You're going to pay for this, I

BEWARE OF DOG!

promise you that! You better not let me catch you sleeping!" Stacey screamed as the bailiff dragged her from the courtroom.

I didn't want Stacey's money. I'd raise the kids the best way that I knew how. I knew that it was going to take a lot of help from family and friends to watch the kids, but I was going to be the best father that I could possibly be. Besides that, I wanted to be the best man that I could be. Not just for the kids, but for me. I had made so many mistakes, and Lord only knew if He'd forgive me, but I was determined that this was a promise that I was going to keep for me and my children, right?

BEWARE OF DOG!

Part III

One year later...

A little closure

BEWARE OF DOG!

"He who is born a fool is never cured."
—African proverb

Chapter 28

Xavier

I always viewed Stacey as a good mother, but now I just view her as a witch from hell. Wouldn't you know that she hasn't seen the kids in a year? Justin asks for her constantly, and I struggle with his behavior on a regular basis. Just last week I had to go up to his school for the fifth time in one month. He's always getting into fights with kids for what appears to be no apparent reason and he's even becoming violent toward his little sister and disrespectful to me, which, of course, I'm not having that. Trust me, I see it all of the time with these kids out on the streets. It's definitely a cry for help. I think it's safe to say that I've finally learned what's significant in life. God, my children and my health are all extremely important to me. How my children view me is also essential. I've finally learned to stop thinking with my smaller head and have finally cut the ties to all of these valueless women. Troi and I have had a few conversations, here and there, but there was no way that a meaningful relationship between the two of us could have ever been formulated. Look at how it all began. All on the basis of lies, destruction and deceit. Sounds like a

BEWARE OF DOG!

juicy novel.

Anyway, I'm good. Things for me could definitely be worse. My mother-in-law helps me out with Ayanna and Justin, and she even took an early retirement package so that she could be there for the children on the nights that I have to work late. I have a great support system, so I keep on moving. Every dog will have her day. So, it should come as no surprise to you when Stacey got her just due and it just so happened that the whole city of Philadelphia was able to see it all unfold.

According to the newspapers, apparently Captain Christine Willis had been allegedly harassing a police officer by the name of Kimberly West. When Stacey learned that Chris was interested in another woman, she approached Officer West to find out what was going on. When Officer West told Stacey that she wasn't interested in Chris, in fact she wasn't interested in women at all, Stacey then tried to convince her to drop the sexual harassment charges. When Officer West refused, Stacey then began leaving threatening messages on the woman's home phone. Once Officer West heard the messages, she reported Stacey to the Internal Affairs Division and the granted an interview to the local newspaper about sexual harassment in the police department.

The newspaper conducted a follow-up story and reported that Stacey and Chris were placed on administrative action, pending the outcome of the investigation. After the article ran, a week later, there was a report of the late night news that Stacey used a police cruiser and ran it into the back of Officer West's personal vehicle—with her kids in it nonetheless. Stacey was charged with aggravated assault and was subsequently removed from her role in the police department.

She's been calling lately to speak to the children and I'll have to be honest, I had to truly pray on this, especially since

BEWARE OF DOG!

she contacted her mother and asked for my number. I truly felt sorry for Stacey because her mother told me she lost the baby while she was going through that whole ordeal.

I've finally gotten Justin to see that he's loved by both of his parents and it's no fault of his own that all of this happened between Stacey and me. Sometimes I do think that most, if not all of this was my fault. If I hadn't ever stepped out on my marriage then Stacey would have never been forced to lead a life outside of our marriage, but we all make our own choices and I can't take all of the blame. My partner, Clinton, and his wife, Teresa finally convinced me to attend Clinton's men's fellowship classes. Clinton is a deeply religious Pentecostal and they were a little overpowering for me, just beginning out and all. So, although I attend the meetings whenever I can, I have begun going to a church called Bethel Presbyterian, located in North Philly. I like the word of Reverend Stratton, the atmosphere and the fact that everyone in there is not a holy roller. I don't think I'll ever be considered as a J.J. (Jesus Junior), but at least I'm a better man than I was one year ago. Who could ask for much more, right?

BEWARE OF DOG!

"God doesn't shut a door without first opening a window."
—Author unknown

Chapter 29

Troi

Looking back to last year, I can hardly believe that I'm single again. My practice has finally expanded. I've just added two new partners and business is doing better than ever. Sadly it seems that I'm doing better as a single woman than I did as an almost married one. I guess the old saying, "I can do bad by myself" is true. Who would have ever thought that to be the case? I've been getting a series of hangups lately at the office and I know that it's Malcolm. I got a postcard from Mexico last week and it had the numbers 458 on it, which is the code Malcolm and I used whenever we wanted to beep each other to say, "I love you." Please! I'm not even thinking about him. I know a year is not really that long and I should still be mourning about the demise of my relationship, but it's apparent that Malcolm never truly loved me in the first place. How would you explain him just picking up and leaving me at the drop of a dime and turning out to be a brotha on the down low? I don't call that love.

I have a friend who wanted to hook me up with his

BEWARE OF DOG!

partner, Carl Singleton. He's also a lawyer here in Philadelphia. We've been emailing each other and he sent me a picture of himself, and I was definitely pleased with his appearance. He is a recent divorcee, but has an eight year old daughter. From what he explained, he doesn't have any drama with his ex-wife and that was fine with me 'cause I can definitely live without that. Now, I know that the last thing in the world that I should be thinking about is getting romantically involved with some man, but it's been one year. What's a girl supposed to do?

While rummaging through some old business cards I ran across Gavin's number. The guy I met in New York. I can't believe he never called me. I guess that was a blessing in disguise. I started to dial his number and then thought it was better to leave well enough alone.

I ran into Xavier last week at family court and he was telling me all about his situation with his ex-wife. In fact, I had read about all of the drama in the newspaper, and I was definitely glad that we had decided to end things between us before an even crazier situation developed. Sometimes I wonder if what happened to Malcolm and me was a result of the old saying, "What goes around comes around." The fact that Xavier and I had even cheated may be the very same reason that my own relationship dissolved. But, I can't live in the past I have to move on and at least learn from my mistakes. I know that there were many things that I could have done differently but nobody's perfect. Thankfully, I still do believe in marriage, love and happiness and all of that other stuff that Al Green used to sing about. When or if I ever do find someone to love me, I now know what it takes to be a great wife, right?

"Peace is costly but worth the expense."
—African proverb

Chapter 30

Corie

There is no way in hell that I can marry Lance. Not now, not ever. For one, I finally met his parents and they are the most uppity folks that I've ever encountered. You see, I thought that I knew Lance, and for the most part I did. I saw in him what he wanted me to see. You really don't know someone until you see how they're living all they way around. That's exactly why I now realize that when you're creepin' on the down low you feel like you've hit the jackpot.

Here's my theory. Let's take a man and he's been happily married for about ten years. The wife begins to view her husband as boring and tired, and she's just plain sick of being in his company. Her husband doesn't bring anything new and exciting to the marriage and frankly, she begins to resent coming home to him every night. But, for whatever reason, she decides she doesn't want to leave the family home, so she begins to creep with a man she met at work. This man is single, no kids and for the most part, he's the best thing in the world to her. He knows his situation at home and any free sex he can get without any strings attached is just fine with him. Each time

BEWARE OF DOG!

they see each other, she's decked out in her Friday night best, he always has the house clean and is always available and ready for his new woman, but neither of them is keeping it real. She's wearing her hair in a fancy new style and has taken off her ripped drawers, only to replace them with her new Victoria's Secret thong and he always has on his designer silk boxers. She's always freshly polished with her manicure and pedicure and all of her fancy lingerie.

Again, neither of them is doing what they would normally do, but they're both giving all they've got. The woman's husband, on the other hand, has slipped into a pattern of simplicity and comfort and he's gained a few pounds around the midsection and he's wearing his ripped boxers to bed. He's also working long hours because his wife wants to live the good life, so he's neglected to send flowers and take her out to dinner while he continues at an effortless pace to try and make her happy. After all, no person can make you happy, except you, but she doesn't realize this and constantly complains that she just isn't happy anymore.

When I look back at my situation with Lance, I realize that we just didn't know each other. We were doomed from the start. I saw Lance the way I wanted and needed to see him. When we had dinner with his mother, they asked me a series of questions about my background and my lineage, and I think the look on my face said it all. If there is one thing that I can't stand, it's a bourgeois person. It doesn't matter what color you are, but it seems like it's a little tougher pill to swallow when it's a person of color. As descendants of slaves, we all came here the same way—on ships. So, please tell me where we went wrong that we turn up our noses on one another because some of us have advanced to a higher income than others. I know that in societies, you're always going to have lower, middle and, high-income families, but having money and lots of it doesn't mean you have to be snooty and think you're better than someone else. Hell, my mother is a member of Links, a member of Delta Sigma Theta Sorority and she and my dad own their own computer consulting business, so they have a nice bit of change, but I've just never been exposed to people who think they're better than others. When I saw Lance not taking up for me and allowing his uppity-ass mother to attempt to climb all up my family tree I looked at him in a completely different light. We had the biggest argument right in front of his mom, which I know wasn't appropriate, but I just couldn't help myself. Lance's mother was asking me all of these questions about my parents coming over to America and asking me what schools they attended and I just flipped.

"Why is that so important where and what schools my parents attended?"

"I'm just asking, dear. I'm a member of Alpha Kappa Alpha Sorority, and I may know some of the same people your parents know," Mrs. Jackson said.

"I doubt that. My mother and I are both members of the illustrious sorority, Delta Sigma Theta."

"Oh, I see. You chose the second best. You do realize that AKA is the first black Greek sorority, founded on the campus of Howard University in 1908, dear," Mrs. Jackson stated with a pursed lip.

"Yes, and then came the Deltas. There were twenty-two founding members who saw a need for an organization that provided community service and less social functions."

"Oh my, I see you're confused. The AKAs are notable today for the work that we provide to the community."

"You're absolutely right. Both sororities as well at the other seven black Greek organizations do tremendous work.

BEWARE OF DOG!

There's room for all of us," I stated as I tried to call a truce.

"Dear, are you a member of any other women's organizations?" Mrs. Jackson asked.

"My cousin is a member of the New Castle County chapter of The Charmettes, Inc. and I'm trying to begin a chapter in Philadelphia, but I've been really busy lately. It's a goal that I'm working on for this year."

"Surely you don't have idle time to spend on less prestigious organizations. You need to attend some of my social meetings. I'm sure that you'll want to get out of that nightclub business when you settle down with my Lance."

"I think you have me all wrong. I don't plan to scale down my business. In fact, we're looking to sell this club and begin expanding some place else," I stated.

"My heavens. For the life of me I can't see how you could surround yourself with those people who fill those horrible clubs. Listening to that gangster rap music and goodness knows what else that goes on in there."

"Why don't you ask your son? You do realize that he's one of my key investors."

"What? Lance is this what you're doing with your inheritance money? I see when your father returns home from Paris we'll have to have a long discussion," Mrs. Jackson stated.

"Yes, mom," Lance said quietly.

"Correct me if I'm wrong, but isn't that Lance's money to do what he pleases?"

"Young lady, I'll thank you to stay out of our family affairs. This doesn't concern you."

"Obviously it does. When Lance and I get married, his money will be mine and vice versa. So, it is my business."

"Lance, surely you've talked to her about what we discussed. You did tell her about the prenuptial agreement,"

BEWARE OF DOG!

Mrs. Jackson stated.

The look on Lance's face said it all. I knew right then and there that he was never who I thought he was. What he was a spineless, wanna-be-gangsta—a wangsta.

I stormed out of there and went back to Lance's suite. I packed up all of my clothes and as I was leaving he came strolling in.

"My mom is trippin'. As you can see she's high strung. None of us pays any attention to anything she says. You've got to know how not to push her buttons."

"It's over. I realized tonight that I really don't know you at all. I need some space so that I can clear my head."

"I know you're not going to break up with me over this."

"When you cut the cord from your mommy, holla at ya girl. Until then, business is business, but you've got to stand up for me and I don't think you know how to do that."

"I've given up a lot for you. I can't lose my family too. I want you in my life and I don't want to lose you," Lance said.

"You just did. I can't be the man and the woman in this relationship, Lance. When you choose between your family or me, let me know," I said, walking past Lance and out the door.

Knowing me I won't go back. It's pointless. A sista's on the move. Once I'm out, I'm out. I through with dating for a while. Right now, I just want to focus on finding me new business opportunities, my family and me. The rest will all fall into place. If you see me at the club, holla at me because I may be back, right?

Acknowledgments

First and foremost, I'd like to thank God for rescuing and continuing to carry me. I'd also like to thank God for my angels on earth and the people in my life who make me complete.

I am not going to thank the entire world this time around, even though I know that friends like to see their names in books. You'll just have to know that I love each and every one of you and that your name is written on my heart. Okay, I do need to thank my family and very close friends. I'll attempt to make this short. I'd like to thank the: Lewis, Simmons, Hanton, and Bradley families. You've all contributed to who I am, in some way, shape or form. I'd also like to thank my good friends, Diana Santiago, Barbara Inman, Al Channel, Rondetta Beck, Teresa Westbrooks, Eugenia Glenn, Donna Taylor, Dianna Jefferson, Rhonda Kennedy, Vanita Evans, Lourdes Marques, L. Jeffrey Green, Tony Baylor, James LaVar Ransome (keep your head up), Dennis Carpenter Jones and his family.

My earth angels: Reverend and Mrs. Jimmy L. Stratton. My sister, Ghaka and her Sweet family. My niece, Taylor and my nephew A.J., my sister Sherrilia and her family, my brother Devon and his family, my aunt Shirley, my cousin Leslie, Uncle Thomas and Aunt Cynthia, Sherrie Boddie, Kayla, and Tray Boddie and all of my other family members, which are too great to list.

My Charmette friends and family, and my dear friend Sharia Hudson and family.

A special thanks to my wonderful Sorors and beautiful line sisters of Fusion, of the Wilmington (DE) Chapter of Delta Sigma Theta Sorority, Incorporated.

I can't forget to thank Ms. Joan Thompkins and her

family. Thanks for all that you've done for me.

To the great authors that I've met along the way: Azarel, T. Wendy Williams, Daaimah Poole, Travis Hunter, Michael Presley, Crystal Lacey Winslow, Marcus Major, Dorothy Goins, Shauna Grundy and Natalie Darden and all of the other great writers. Keep up the great work. Thanks to Between the Lines Book Club, for feeding me and my girl, Diana, and welcoming us in to your hearts, homes and your conversations. Thanks all other book clubs throughout the country—thanks for the mad love and support.

I can't forget my editor, Chandra Sparks Taylor. Thanks so much for your guidance, professionalism, and expertise.

I'd also like to thank my first woman, my mommy. You are the bomb and don't ever let anyone tell you otherwise. You did a fine job (if I must say so myself). I'll always love you! I wish I could give you the world—it would be yours.

Finally, I wish to close this book out by thanking the love of my life, my other woman—Courtney—my daughter, my friend, my everything. You make mommy proud to even know you. That doesn't mean you can't work a nerve like nobody's business, but I love you just the same. Know that I'll always be there for you—when I'm gone. You just have no idea of the power of my love for you. Your father and I expect nothing but the absolute best from you. You're loved by us both.

Thanks to all of the people that purchased my book(s) (now stop sharing and buy your own) and those who continue to inspire me to write. I truly know that this is my calling.

Again, thanks and I look forward to getting even better, each time around.

Book Club Discussion Questions

1. Xavier started off as a real player. Do you think his transformation was believable? Can a man like this truly change?

2. Stacey fell in love with Chris. Do you think she always had feelings for women, or do you think Xavier's ways pushed her to this point?

3. Troi started off not believing in cheating on her man, yet she was so easily strayed by Gavin. Why do you think this was the case?

4. Corie only dates men who are married and thugs. Do you think the reason she was so hardcore was because she lost her son and she was bitter?

5. Do you think the title should have been, Men Experiment Women Cheat? Why or why not?

6. Malcolm told Troi that he wasn't gay, yet he likes the flavor of men every now and then. Does this make him gay, bisexual or both?

7. Down low brothers are on the rise and African American women are becoming infected with HIV at alarmingly high rates. What, if anything can be done to stop this epidemic?